Dedicated to....

What Winning the World Series Means to Chicago White Sox Fans

WhiteSoxInteractive.com

Edited by George Bova

authorHOUSE™

1663 Liberty Drive, Suite 200
Bloomington, Indiana 47403
(800) 839-8640
www.AuthorHouse.com

First published by AuthorHouse 11/30/05

ISBN: 1-4259-0187-5 (sc)

Printed in the United States of America
Bloomington, Indiana

This book is printed on acid-free paper.

Foreword

By Bill Pierce with Mark Liptak

"World Champions ... can you believe it!" That was my first thought as I was watching Juan Uribe fire to Paul Konerko to record the final out in the 2005 World Series. Right after that, I thought of our shortstop, Luis Aparicio, and that night in Cleveland so many years ago when he started the double play that gave us the 1959 pennant. Absolute elation ... hard to believe.

As the season went along and it looked like the 2005 White Sox were about to make history, a lot of the former players on the 1959 team, like Jim Landis, Bob Shaw, and me, would get media requests for interviews, and one thing we were always asked was how this year's team compared to ours.

It was amazing how close the two teams were. Both clubs won with the staples of baseball: great pitching and great defense. Back in my time, we had a very good pitching staff. We had the starters in Early Wynn, Bob Shaw, Dick Donovan, and myself. We had "Turk" Lown and Gerry Staley in the bullpen. This year's team also had a deep, talented staff. When you have pitchers like Mark Buehrle, Jon Garland, Jose Contreras, Freddy Garcia, and Dustin Hermanson, you're going to win a lot of games. Both teams had great defenses, particularly up the middle. We had Sherm Lollar behind the plate, Aparicio and Nellie Fox in the infield, and Landis in center field. The 2005 club had A.J. Pierzynski at catcher, Uribe and Tad Iguchi at short and second, and Aaron Rowand in center. Believe me, those guys could catch the baseball.

The two clubs also played and won a number of one-run games. Those are the kind of games you see in the playoffs. As a fan, it was tough watching those kinds of games! It takes a lot out of you ... so much so that at the end, when it's over, you are physically drained.

There were only two differences between the clubs. One was that the 2005 version had a lot more power than we did. They hit two hundred home runs. We didn't come close to that. The other difference was the styles of the managers. Al Lopez, who recently passed away, was a quiet man. He told us what he wanted then worked through his assistant coaches. Ozzie Guillen, this year's manager, was always involved in something. He was always with the players ... talking, joking, having fun. I'm not saying one is right and the other wrong. They just had different styles.

I understand that the proceeds from this book are going to the Chicago Baseball Cancer Charities. I've been involved with this organization since I was first invited to play in a golf tournament back in 1970. For the past fifteen years, I've been the chairman. I can tell you that the organization makes a real difference in helping combat this disease that in one way or another has touched all of us. For me, it took my former roommate of eleven years, Nellie Fox, and it also took my catcher for so many years, Sherm Lollar.

The organization had its roots back in the early '70s when it was known as The Hutch Fund, named after the late baseball manager of the Reds Fred Hutchinson. I saw the good that this organization and the people who devoted so much of their time was doing, and I wanted to be a part of it. Over the years, the organization has raised around eleven and a half million dollars for cancer research. We hold a yearly golf outing and an auction that raises money, and we also get a number of donations from different groups, individuals, and professional businesses.

The White Sox themselves, under Chairman Jerry Reinsdorf, have helped tremendously over the years. I can't thank them enough for all of their assistance and support. They have devoted time and energy to our cause, and in many cases, White Sox players themselves, very quietly, have come to visit the children who are fighting this illness. A number of the Cubs players, including Kerry Wood, have also participated and brought smiles to the children and their parents. At least for a few hours, the difficult times are forgotten as fans of all ages are able to meet and talk with their heroes.

Our fund goes directly to cancer research and cancer care. We work particularly with Northwestern Hospital and the Children's Memorial Hospital in the Chicago area. In addition, during the summer, we send a number of children up to Wisconsin. There, at Camp One-Step-At-A-Time, they have the chance to just be kids, having fun in the woods, swimming, and playing games including baseball, which all kids do.

I've spoken with the doctors on a number of occasions, and they have all told me how much this money that we raise helps them. It enables them to treat cancer today, and it also funds the research that's needed to learn more about it for the future. The goal is still the same and always will be: to eliminate cancer in all forms, completely.

To all those groups and organizations that contribute and have contributed over the years, I sincerely thank you. I also thank the individuals who give their time, efforts, and money to help. I can't possibly name all of them, but some in particular that I want to acknowledge are Gene Hiser, former major league player Bob Miller, Dick Schramm, Marv Samuels, and former big league pitcher Don Elston.

I was asked by Mark to whom I would dedicate this 2005 World Championship. My answer is simply to all those true White Sox fans, those who have waited so long and for so many years, those who have lived and died with this team. Finally, right now, all of us can say, "We did it!"

Bill Pierce
Chairman, Chicago Baseball Cancer Charities

Introduction

Proud of Our Champion Sox

More than the fans of any other professional sports franchise in America, Chicago White Sox fans have a unique love/hate relationship with their team. A confused mythology has emerged about what we Sox fans feel— or don't feel—for our team. The Sox are the second team in the second city, a team with over eighty years of championship futility, but the story of the team's fan base remained a mystery. Though the years of frustration stretched the limits of every living Chicagoan's memory, the Sox's years of futility were still only second best. Sox fans' allegiance endured, but the wider world mostly ignored them.

Now the outside world can't ignore our story any longer. A certain type of fan in Chicago refused to accept mediocrity. A certain type of fan in Chicago refused to be sucked in by media hype and fake tradition. A certain type of fan in Chicago stood up and declared that winning—and nothing else—was worthy of supporting. Sox fans are unique in Chicago.

Who are these Sox fans? What makes them line the streets through six Chicago neighborhoods, jam the sidewalks and side streets up and down LaSalle Street, and bless their own sweet fortune for having witnessed what they feared they might never live to see—a Sox World Series Championship?

The confused mythology wasn't a problem for Sox fans; we always knew what we were about. Spend ten minutes surfing the Internet fan Web site White Sox Interactive (www.whitesoxinteractive.com), and anyone willing to learn about Sox fans certainly won't be confused any longer. It's the biggest such Web site devoted to Sox fans on the Internet, and an unmistakable voice emerges: We care deeply about winning, and we ought not be underestimated.

White Sox Interactive stands as a testament for what we know ourselves to be. While Americans gave thanks for their blessings on Thanksgiving Day back in 1998 and settled in front of the TV for a few hours of football, the very first pages of White Sox Interactive were coded and launched. It was only five pages, but its birth on the high holiday of American football speaks to the passion that Sox fans know for their team.

A Sox fan's passion for winning knows no season, whether the team wins one hundred ten games like they did in 2005 or only seventy-five like in 1999. Now seven years later, dozens of new features on topics as diverse as Disco Demolition and a pictorial tribute to Old Comiskey Park (both the largest of their kind on the Internet) reside with hundreds more stories, reports, and columns. Through thousands of contributions and posts from around the country and around the globe, the voice of Sox fandom is manifest at White Sox Interactive.

In just one simple message board thread, the story emerges of what individual Sox fans feel about the 2005 season and the team of heroes who delivered the one and only true triumph worth possessing: a Chicago baseball championship. No true student of Sox fandom could ever doubt that this is the prize that drives us to be Sox fans.

The dedications are diverse, over four hundred total. Read them and listen closely. Hear the voices of the hundreds of Sox fans who wrote them. But you'll also hear the voices of the Sox fans this championship is dedicated to—mothers and fathers, aunts, uncles, and cousins who instilled in these Sox fans a lifelong love for baseball and the team; brothers, sisters, friends, and sometimes just acquaintances who lived to share lasting memories at the ballpark but didn't live to witness this triumph except in the hearts of the Sox fans dedicating it to their memory.

After eighty-eight years of waiting, not every Sox fan lived to witness this moment. However, every living Sox fan knows and remembers those who passed on, and we feel twice-blessed to carry their memory inside us at this moment. After all, we Sox fans attend their funerals and visit their final resting places, and we Sox fans alone carry their memory at this crowning moment. That's the sort of perspective you won't find in any other Sox championship book.

That's what makes this book of dedications so special. Professional writers didn't write it, though WSI has quite a few of them. Chicago and national media reporters didn't write it, though many of them "lurk" at WSI and a few of them even post. The voice that emerges in this book is the voice of Sox fans who understand what this Sox championship represents. It might be the only place in which the outside world can hear so clearly what we feel at this very moment in time.

It's a damned good story. We're proud of our champion Sox. Now take a moment and learn why.

- George Bova
- Editor and founder,
- White Sox Interactive

~~~~~~

White Sox Interactive is 100 percent staffed by Sox fan volunteers working for the love of the team and the sport. Visit WSI on the World Wide Web at www.flyingsock.com or www.whitesoxinteractive.com.

One hundred percent of the editor's proceeds from this book are being donated to Billy Pierce's Chicago Baseball Cancer Charities. A portion of the publisher's proceeds is being donated, too. Learn more about Billy Pierce's Chicago Baseball Cancer Charities at www.chicagobaseballcc.org.

Dedicated to ...my grandpa (we called him "papaw"), a man from the greatest generation of Americans.

This man stormed Normandy with a Sox pennant in his pack. He was that big a fan. It was one of the only things he just WOULD NOT part with.

He raised my father a Sox fan, and I was the third generation. I have that old man to thank ... the original. A guy who moved to Chicago as a teenager and became a Sox fan sometime in the mid 1930s. He died in 1990, never getting to see the moment that we just saw.

This one's for you, Grandpa.

Here's to all of the true believers out there. Generations of people have waited so patiently for this moment, and it is upon us. Congratulations to all Sox fans. This is our moment in the sun. GO SOX!

—Jurr

Dedicated to ...

I do not in ANY WAY intend to bring down the excitement of today's celebrations. I just wanted to address all of those Sox fans who aren't with us today. I for one know growing up on the North Side I wouldn't be a Sox fan had it not been for my dad. So wherever you're at today, Dad, I hope you and Grandpa are enjoying this as much as you and I did in 2000 and 1993. I was only a year old in 1983.

I'll never forget that 2000 season with my dad as long as I live. We've got a neighbor who's on the Sox (can't say who), and we had great seats and parking that year.

Was anyone else at the game last Sunday? I've been to a few games after my dad died, but this one was extremely emotional for some reason. They played the "best of 2005 clips" on the scoreboard prior to the game, and for some reason I just teared up. I thought it was pretty cool that Paulie, A.J, Rowand, and some other players stood out on the field and watched it as well. Something in the air that game!

—**Bill Aqua**

Dedicated to . . .my old man, who passed away back in February. He is the reason why I am a Sox fan!

—**PINWHEELS**

Dedicated to . . .my professional mentor who chided me (he was a Clevelander). Boy, I wish I could chide him right now. He passed on in March.

—**Hokiesox**

Dedicated to . . .my grandfather who is a Royals fan to whom I cheered against just to spite him, which eventually turned me into being a die-hard Sox fan. UH-OH, DJ is the man!

—**antitwins13**

Dedicated to . . .my uncle, who took me to Sox games when I was a kid back in Indiana, died last month. He never got to see a Sox championship. Hopefully he'll get to see one real soon from somewhere up there.

Thanks, Sox.
—Sxy Mofo

Dedicated to . . .

I'm sure a lot of us owe our allegiance to our ancestors. My Grandma Boyd has been dead for more than 30 years and my dad for 23, but I have no doubt they're up there right now—probably drinking a Bud with Little Nell and dancing an Irish jig!

Allow me to join you!

Had to add my brother Bobby Boyd, my partner in crime, with whom I spent many years going to Comiskey when we were teenagers, hopping on the El after school. The day after the Sox won the 2005 Series, he e-mailed me that he still wasn't totally convinced we'd win!

THAT's a Sox fan!

My dad, Rollo Boyd, would have been 83 on October 28, 2005, the day of the rally. And I'm getting the wobbly chin again, on his behalf.

—MarySwiss

Dedicated to . . .my grandmother who raised my dad a Sox fan which was passed on to me. One of my fave parts of visiting Chi-town as a youngster was knowing that after the 12-hour drive from hell every summer she'd have the game on the TV for me and fill me in on what I'd missed.

—DC Sox Fan

Dedicated to . . .the long list of great Sox fans before us ...

Please add my dad, who shared his love of all things Sox with me, until I was 19. Dad passed away suddenly on 1/27/83. I'm told the last conversation he had was about an off-season Sox trade. I was so torn apart I couldn't bear to watch one pitch in 1983 and missed the entire season. He would be ECSTATIC today.

—BarbG

Dedicated to . . .my dad who, when I was seven years old, whipped out a newspaper from October 1st, 1956, with the news of Don Larsen's no-hitter on the back page. This made me a baseball fan. Then he took out the paper with the headline that stated the Sox had clinched in '59. He also showed me the many ticket stubs he had collected from his going to games that year. This made me a Sox fan. He died one month before the new Sox park would open. I love you, DAD. And I miss you.

—flo-B-flo

4

Dedicated to . . .

In 1983 we stood in line at Comiskey all night long to get playoff tickets. Rob kept us laughing, and around dawn he went for doughnuts. Gone way too young— may perpetual light shine upon him.

—SoxandtheCityTee

Dedicated to . . . my grandfather, John; one of the original dark clouds is watching this and smiling wide. He taught an entire family to root for the Sox, and we are carrying on his legacy in style.

My aunt Georgeanna, who was taken way too soon from us is smiling at her daughter who is as big a Sox fan as any one of us and has to do deal with all of the Yankee fans she lives near. I hope this gives her some joy as well.

To all of those Sox fans who are thinking of family and friends departed, drink one tonight in honor of them.

For John and Anna.

Go Sox.

—OzzieBall

Dedicated to . . . my grandpa Rocco, who took me to every home game as a kid. He introduced me to the scorecard, the hot-dog, and sweet sound of "Harold, Harold!"

2005 White Sox: Win or die trying!

I don't want to die.

—bigdommer

Dedicated to . . . my mom, who will have passed away way too young three years ago on October 8th. My brother and I took her to the clincher in '93, and I really miss watching games with her or calling her and asking her what she's doing and getting the reply, "Watching the game."

Hopefully God will give all of our folks that have moved on to better things a few hours off from strumming their harps so they can watch the playoffs with us.

[Whew. Good cry. I think I needed that.]

—Realist

Dedicated to . . . my dad, who was around back in 1959 but never saw them win the World Series. He passed away last year on 5/15 after we watched the White Sox vs. Twins. Rarely did we ever get a chance to watch a Saturday night game together, since he was usually at work.

—ChiWhiteSox1337

Dedicated to ...

I hoist a glass to toast my late father (Red) who died on July 13, 1977 (the night of the famous NY City black-out). I inherited his love of the game and the White Sox. (Ironically I was at the Sox game the night he died!)

I'll always have a mental image of my father watching the Sox on the old b/w TV out on the back porch after a long day's work and watching them battle the hated Yankees for the pennant.

Also to my wife's father Rich who died July 18, 1988. Two men who loved their White Sox and passed the torch on down to their children.

Thanks, Dads ... for everything. This celebration would be that much sweeter if you were here to enjoy it with us. But I feel you already are!

—Wsoxmike59

Dedicated to ... Nellie Fox, Sherm Lollar, Ted Kluszewski, Bubba Phillips, Billy Goodman, Dick Donovan, Early Wynn, Al Smith, as well as the living icons Billy Pierce, Minnie Minoso, Jim Landis, and all who made it easy and fun to be a White Sox fan. To Bob Elson and Jack Brickhouse for filling my ears with wonderful moments and telling me the history of the game as they saw it. Lastly, to my dad who introduced me to the game and made me a lifelong fan.

—chisox59

Dedicated to ...my dad, who was the only Sox fan in a sea of Cubs fan relatives. And to my grandpa, who was as much of a die-hard fan as I am! Thanks for teaching me to be a Sox fan and taking me to Sox games at Old Comiskey. I wore my late father's hat to the final home game on Sunday! I will cherish that hat forever. To the 2005 Sox. Thanks for a great summer!! Keep it going through October!

—chisoxfanforever

Dedicated to ...my dad and grandpa; thanks for being SOX fans. And to all SOX fans present and past.

Dad, you always said, "Son, have patience and your dreams will come true." Well, you were right; the SOX are in the World Series. Even though you are no longer with us, you are sharing in this victory.

—soxjim

Dedicated to ...

Words cannot describe the feelings I have right now after watching the team I have followed for thirty years finally grasp the Brass Ring, a feat that I sometimes wondered if I would ever see. Thank you, Uncle Jerry, for steering me on the right course early; you took me to see the Sox at Old Comiskey and bitched about Bill Veeck trading away all his decent players. It's a shame you couldn't be around when they finally accomplished the goal. I did the next best thing; I wore your hat from 1977 for the final game of the World Series.

—Daver

Dedicated to ...my grandpa, who was a Sox fan very possibly from their start (he was born in 1889) and who told me stories about Ed Walsh, Joe Jackson, and the guy who seemed to me to be his personal favorite, Buck Weaver. When he died in 1972, the Sox were about to re- verse their fortunes

with Dick Allen, but he didn't live to see it. And to my dad who wasn't a huge fan but at least took me to my first Sox games and tolerated my fanaticism.

"I told you there weren't any curses!"

—Torn Labrum

Dedicated to ...my sister Sarah who we just lost to leukemia in Au- gust. Not the biggest baseball fan in the world ... but allowed me to convince all three of my great nieces/ nephews to be White Sox fans ... and always let me take everyone to a Sox game when they were visiting from Iowa.

She would have been the first one to call me this afternoon.

Also Dedicated to …
Luke Appling
Nellie Fox
Luis Aparicio
Billy Pierce
Al Lopez
Bill Veeck
Charley Lau
Loren Babe

—TomBradley72

Dedicated to …my maternal grandpa, who I remember sitting on the couch with and watching the Sox with back in the late '80s. He taught me the very basics of baseball—what the R-H-E means in the line score, what a line score even was, and the other basics of the game—and I know he's got to be so proud. He died in 1990 when I was just 10½ years old, so this is the third division championship he's missed, but this is, by far, the most special and the one I think he would've enjoyed the most. When I last visited his grave in July, I said a special prayer to him, thinking to myself, "Grandpa, this season is for you. We're winnin' it all this year."

WHITE SOX: 2005 WORLD CHAMPIONS!

I've waited all my life for this and it means more to me than I can say. I never stopped believin'!

—ChiSoxGirl

Dedicated to ...my 92-year-old grandmother who is still here to see and to her brother, my Uncle Bud (my grandma's younger brother), the man who encouraged the love of the White Sox in me, my brother (our father is not much of a baseball fan), my uncles, and my cousins. He never had a lot of money but had season tickets at Old Comiskey for many years. He took me to a bunch of Sox games. He never saw a White Sox World Series victory in his lifetime (he was born in 1919 and died a few years back), but he always remained faithful to the team, even when the organization took away the seats he had as a season ticket holder for the 1983 playoffs. Like my grandma, he was a lifelong South Sider (born in the South Side of Chicago, later spent many years in the suburb of Riverdale, where he first lived with my mom's family and later his own). He gave me my first piece of Sox memorabilia (a team poster of the 1982 White Sox team, which hung on my bedroom wall for several years until my mother decided to throw it out). He made me a White Sox fan. Every time the Sox do well, I think of him (along with my grandma, who is, thankfully, still with us and still following the White Sox, and who, despite living in a retirement home on the North Side, still proudly declares herself a South Sider).

—Uncle_Patrick

Dedicated to ...my dad, who took my brother and I to Sox games since they were at night while my mom took us to Cubs games since they were during the day (unfortunately my sister chose the dark side). But we were there in '83 on the night they clinched a tie for the West title, and 2½ years later he passed away from brain cancer. I remember having a lot of similar thoughts in the last night game at the old park as the fireworks show was going on. I'm just glad he made sure my brother and I had plenty of chances to see the right team on the right side of town.

—**nordhagen**

Dedicated to ...my dad, who was a huge basketball fan (Lakers of the '70s and '80s, Bulls of the '80s and '90s), but nonetheless, found the time to take me to my first game in 1983. He was as excited when Fisk hit a walk-off shot as I was. It's a moment I'll never forget.

Love you, Dad, and I miss you.

Chicago White Sox: *Forgotten* no more.

2005 World Series Champions.

—**ChiSox14305635**

Dedicated to ...

Dear 2005 Chicago White Sox,

Congrats. You guys have put together an awesome season and gave every SOX fan an amazing ride already. I am writing because I want you to know how much could be won in the playoffs. My grandpa is 80 years old and a lifelong die-hard SOX fan. He definitely gives me an interesting perspective on things. South Side fans have not had anything to gloat about for his whole lifetime. Please give it all in the playoffs. This is all I ask ...

Sincerely,
jeremydavid

Dedicated to ...my grandfather, who was 30 years in old in 1959. When the Sox lost that year, he probably thought there would be other chances to see the team make the World Series in his lifetime. Unfortunately, he died in 1997 and never got another opportunity. My father was six years old in '59. He also never got another chance. He died in 2003.

Even though I'm only 29, I'm going to make sure I enjoy this playoff run because you never know when it might be the last time you see something like this. For many of us, this is an opportunity to erase three or four generations of losing and frustration in our families. Let's hope that our time is now.

Seize the day, and go Sox!!!

—JB98

Dedicated to ...my dad, who passed away suddenly on November 16 last year. He took me to my first Sox game around 1971; I took him to his last one last June. Big Sox fan all 78 years! This one is for you!

—DumpJerry

Dedicated to ...my grandma. She may not have been the biggest Sox fan, or baseball fan, but when I was 3 years old, she would wear my dad's Sox hat and pitch to me in the backyard when she was in her fifties (and the unknowing kid I was I made her pick up her leg and wind up like Nolan Ryan). When I was young and had no money, she got us tickets, and she may not have known what was going on or (as she always loved to joke) who was on first, but she knew I did, and I got to see the likes of Harold Baines, Ozzie Guillen, and The Big Hurt, and Rockin Robin as youngsters. We laid her to rest on Valentine's Day 2004. I know wherever she is, she doesn't know who Tadahito Iguchi is or Jose Contreras or Bobby Jenks, but I know it was just as it was when I was a kid; she was happy seeing me this happy.

—Domeshot17

Dedicated to ...Grandpa Scotty. I hope you're watching up there. Lifelong fan, loathed the Cubs, and always loved going to games, even as an old man.

My mom told me a story tonight about how Grandpa took the wife and kids to Comiskey one weekend to sit in the press box area with the rest of the reporters and media (he started out as a young journalist in Joliet, and around the time of his retirement, he was a member of the senior staff at the *Gary Post Tribune*).

And to my grandmother and grandfather, Anne and Forbes, originally from Joliet, who took their young kids to games as children, and persevered through years of losing baseball, never letting their hopes of a World Series winner perish. I only wish they could have been here in 2005 to see this ... the Chicago White Sox in all of their glory.

Let's hear it for those 2005 White Sox! This one is just for you, Grandma and Grandpa! I felt you both watching.

Thank you, White Sox, for some of the happiest moments of my life this season!

GO SOX!!

—DieTrying79

Dedicated to ... Dad, who wasn't a big sports fan, but he used to take me to baseball games as a kid. We went to both flubbie and Sox games—actually more flubbie games, and I kind of grew up a flubs fan.

Still, I made it out and never looked back. Dad never questioned my change, and he really didn't care, but he is a major part of the reason I am such a big sports fan today even if he wasn't. He died in January 1999, and I miss him immensely. He may not care who wins this coming series, and I don't believe he's watching me or the games, but if he is somewhere out there, he's smiling because I'm smiling, and I'm smiling because of the Sox.

Thanks, Dad, and of course ... GO SOX!

Here's to you, Big Frank, the real 2000 MVP, steroid free and living large. Congratulations on the ring.

Congratulations to the World Series Champions 2005 Chicago White Sox!!!

—voodoochile

Dedicated to . . .my mom. She passed away last year. I watched about a million Sox games with her. I think she's looking down watching every pitch with me.

—cbone

Dedicated to . . .Mom, Dad, and Brother!

My mom was the last to go. Last fall of cancer. I was basically the one that took care of her every day. Stopping in two, three, four times a day. Even after the Sox collapsed at the end of the season, she would have the game on every day to the end. Even if it was a lopsided 9-2 score or something like that, she would keep it on.

Sorry you missed this, Mom. At least from down here.

You probably got a better view from up there anyway.

Dedicated to …my White Sox family that is no longer here.

My father, who died in his sleep three years ago.

My brother, who lost his battle with cancer a year and a half ago.

Three big-time Sox fans. I know they had the best seat in the house.

—SoxRulecubsdrool

Dedicated to . . . my grandfather Larson, whom I never knew, but was the first person to come to my mind, but I would be remiss not to mention others.

My father's Aunt Virginia, who was as passionate a White Sox fan as any who ever lived. She was 7 years old in 1917 and died in 1988. My aunt tells the story of how she was at a game with "Aunt Virge" in the 1960s. Mickey Mantle came to the plate. A rather big female Yankee fan stood up and yelled for Mantle to hit a homer. Aunt Virge boomed in her Bea Arthur voice, "Siddown!" and topped it off with a name I won't repeat here. Then there was the time she mentioned the Sox in a restaurant. A stranger overheard her and said, "The Sox? You have to root for the Cubs. The Cubs are Chicago's team, Mary!" This started a loud argument during which she yelled, "Shut up and eat your soup!" The stranger turned out to be Dizzy Dean. When she found out and tried to apologize, he told her, "You stick with the Sox."

There is also my grandmother, who died in 2003. Today would have been her 91st birthday. She was a huge Sox fan until they lost. Then she would carry on about how it was "all fixed." She would often cite 1919 as proof. She was in her glory in 1983. The day after Game 4 she rambled on and on about how "Vegas" had decided who would win and who wouldn't. God, she drove me crazy. Still, I know that if she were alive

17

today, she would be happy. Until the Sox lost the first game in the playoffs, that is. Then everything would be back to being fixed again.

—TommyJohn

Dedicated to . . . my dad, who took me to see the Sox when I was a kid and who taught me that the more you feel something, the more alive you are.

To my grandmother, whose failing eyesight in her later years meant she listened to most games on the radio, but who followed the Sox and enjoyed sparring with me in hot-stove debates.

To my wife's dad, who grew up in East Chicago in the 1920s and would take a series of nickel streetcars and buses from EC to Comiskey Park with his brother and his father to see the Sox.

To Art, a guy I worked with in the '70s who was 40 years older than I was, and who was from the South Side and had great stories about old Sox teams.

All of them are gone now. They're four that were in my life, but for me they're symbolic of the thousands who've gone on with them without being able to join the party.

Here's to you all!

And of course, Bill Veeck. Someone else mentioned his name, but it bears repeating. A guy who understood the magic of baseball and, most importantly, understood White Sox fans.

—tebman

Dedicated to . . . my dad, Brendan, who grew up a couple blocks from Comiskey. He wasn't a big sports fan but used to tell us stories about how he and the neighborhood kids would climb fences on Comiskey's exterior, all the way up to the roof, and sit up there to watch games in the 1940s. "If Mom had known, she would have killed us."

And then a couple times a year, he'd take me to a ballgame at the old park. Those were the most fun times I ever had as a kid.

He died 3 years ago, down here in Dallas, but never lost the South Side in him. So here's to you, Dad, hope you're looking down and enjoying.

—**Saracen**

Dedicated to . . .

How about a hoist for George Burns, the wheelchair-bound fan who passed last summer? I know you're up there, buddy. See if you and my old man who left us on September 28, 1993 (yeah, that date is right; he waited until just after we clinched in '93), can get on a cloud and knock a few balls the White way these next two weeks!

—**tacosalbarojas**

Dedicated to . . . Uncle Jim and Grandpa Bob, who are very pleased I'm sure; now help 'em win it all.

—**Muopsies**

Dedicated to ..."Butch" (1925-2002).

Thanks for making me a Sox fan, Dad. I miss watching the games with you. I'm passing on our love for the Sox to your granddaughters, and this year they have really started to understand what it means to be a Sox fan.

—24thStFan

Dedicated to ...my dad, who is still alive. I would like to publicly acknowledge him. He's more of a Cubs fan, and we took in more than a couple of games at Wrigley. But he was more than willing to oblige me when I stumbled upon the greatness that is the White Sox, and took me to many games there. And he was very excited to go when I invited him to one of the games against the Royals earlier in September.

Gotta love dads who love baseball!

—Xploding Scorbord

Dedicated to ...**my dad and his dad ...**

To my dad (1920-1999), who only saw one World Series in his lifetime.

I remember him calling me into the living room (late '50s and early '60s) whenever an animated Hamms Bear beer commercial was on TV between innings. And I remember sitting out in the backyard with him on hot summer nights listening to Bob Elson.

After the clincher in 1959, he popped opened a Hamms, and he slipped me an ice cream bar to celebrate.

He took me to my first game—a twi-night DH with the Red Sox in 1965. We went to many more, including the final game in Old Comiskey, which was played 15 years ago today.

When I was a teenager and young adult, we had our differences, like all fathers and sons. But when it came to the White Sox, we stood on common ground.

—sageofthesox

Dedicated to . . .Uncle Chester. He was a big, tough (mean when he drank, which was often) SOB who never talked much to anyone. But people used to be amazed at the long conversations he had with me as a nine-year-old kid during family gatherings! He talked to me and treated me like an adult because I knew his passion almost as well as him, the White Sox of course. It was the first time I remember any adult having serious conversations with me, an adult who truly cared what I thought about anything. That alone was so neat, even outside of the subject matter. My dad to this day is amazed at the relationship we had; nobody else ever got through to him. Even his wife!

—Fake Chet Lemon

Dedicated to . . .my great-grandfather for rooting for Luke Appling over 80 years ago, my grandfather, my uncle Myron, and of course my dad (1951-2005), who passed away in January, for making all of us (uncles and cousins) die-hard Sox fans (hence the name).

I won't forget the endless discussions about the Sox. The closest Dad ever got to the feeling of what it might be to win a White Sox Championship was how giddy he and my brother and I were when the flubs blew Game 6 and lost Game 7 in '03.

My brother, whtesoxfan4ever, at our father's memorial, which on that day had bad weather with lake effect snow and wind and icy roads, opened his speech with, "Well, it looks like Dad was given two options today for his memorial. One, he could have a beautiful sunny day or the White Sox could win the pennant. I think we know which one Dad picked." That got a good laugh and cheer from a lot of us.

He was the first thing that came to mind when that final out was made, tears of joy and tears of wishing Dad was here in person, but I know he's celebrating somewhere right now. This is for you, Dad; the Sox finally did it.

2005 World Champion Chicago White Sox.

—4ᵗʰ Gen. Sox Fan

Dedicated to . . . my grandparents—Kate, Murph, Marge, and Pat— Sox fans all. I keep thinking how much they would love this!

To my father, who taught me to love the White Sox, and my brother, my baseball partner-in-crime!

Thank you, Kenny!!!!!!!!!

—robiwho

Dedicated to . . . my grandfather, who was born in 1918—1 year after our last World Series. He stayed overnight with me in 1983 to get playoff tickets and went with me to many games as a child, and I will always remember those great games played by the greatest team, The Chicago White Sox.

I'm sure he'll buy a round in heaven when they win it all!!!

Thank you, 2005 World Champion Chicago White Sox!!!

—SouthSide_HitMen

Dedicated to . . . my grandfather John, who turned my dad into the Sox fan that he is today.

I am making it a point to watch these playoff games with my 83-year-old father. This is going to be a special year.

—ClaudelSleptHere

Dedicated to . . . Grandfather Walter, who was born in 1906 and left us in 1988. He was a second-generation Lithuanian who set the course of our family's following the White Sox. Also, of course, to my mother who left us four years ago.

... Luke Appling, Nellie Fox, Chico Carrasquel, Sherm Lollar, Al Smith, Pat Kelly, Double Duty Radcliffe, Richard J. Daley, Willie Thompson, and all the other members of the White Sox family who are celebrating with us in spirit tonight.

Let us also add Msgr. Ignatius McDermott, "Father Mac," who was a longtime Sox fan before passing away last year.

—Viva Medias B's

Dedicated to . . . my mom, who grew up a couple of blocks from Comiskey Park in the 1920s and passed away in March.

—zeker434

Dedicated to . . .

I had my wife (a good Irish girl from the South Side) read this thread, and she was so moved she asked if she could post something about her grandma, Jean. So here is her "guest post":

When I was 10 or 11 years old, I was in my grandma Jean's bedroom (we had just moved to Glenwood from Riverdale). She was the only one with a TV in the house (a tiny little black and white—this was 1966 or '67 mind you). As I was curling her hair, she was intensely watching a baseball game. I, being clueless to the game of baseball, asked her how she knew who to root for. She looked at me in disbelief and simply said, "The SOX of course." Needless to say I've been a SOX fan ever since. Know you're smiling, Jean, love you!

—24thStFan

Dedicated to …my late grandfather, the Reverend Howard Calvin Shaffer, Jr., who passed on in the spring of '94 ... he was an All-American at West Virginia and a semi-pro pitcher, facing many Negro League teams in the '30s. He thought it was great when my dad started taking us to games on the South Side, where so many of the players he had faced got to showcase their skills at the old park. He also praised my dad for buying scalped playoff tickets for the sold-out Toronto series in '93, just six months before he passed away. My dad had never spent so much money for a sports event, and the Sox lost, but it was worth every penny.

I know he's watching with my late grandmother, Elinor Best, who's pulling for the Yankees, and his second wife (my late step-grandmother), Shirley Kimball, who's pulling for the Red Sox ... he probably feels pulled in several different directions ... but I know that a big part of him is thinking about my dad, my brothers, and me, and how much this means to all of us, and that his heart is with the White Sox this year. Plus, he always loved watching teams with great pitching, and it really can't get much better than the 2005 White Sox!!

Every time I watch a game, I think of him, and I'll be thinking of him now more than ever these next few weeks.

Dedicated to my uncle Charles, who was just diagnosed with Alzheimer's Disease at age 62 (way the **** too early). He and my Dad took me to my first game (an extra inning affair in '84 with Vance Law hitting a walk-off HR). I'll never forget the fireworks and my uncle's excitement. He lives in Virginia, where they didn't have any MLB teams, and always liked the White Sox and applauded my dad and my brothers and me for our loyalty and dedication.

He probably can't remember going to that game, and after all is said and done this post season, may not remember much of 2005 due to the Alzheimer's.

I hope I can send him a newspaper clipping from a significant clinching victory so he can have it as a keepsake.

Uncle Charles was a catcher (and also a cornerback) at Ohio Wesleyan and always had a deep love and reverence for the game, which is still a very special part of his relationship with my dad. This love was passed on seamlessly to my younger brothers and me, as we live in three different cities (Boston, NYC, and Houston) but remain as close as ever.

Also, win it for Ray Schalk, Sherm Lollar, Carlton Fisk, and AJ Pierzynski, and all other catchers who have showed such strong leadership and tenacity over the years.

GO WHITE SOX!! It's OUR turn!!

—**Shafe72**

Dedicated to . . .

One year ago a poster on the Red Sox message board Sonsofsamhorn.com started a thread during the ALCS to urge the other members of the message board, some 1,900 strong, to do the same—urging the Red Sox to win it for the special people in their lives who had loved the team through thick and thin.

From the grateful man who lost his brother in Okinawa 60 years ago to the sibling who dedicated a Sox victory to her brother who perished on September 11, 2001, there were scores of tributes from the populace of Red Sox Nation, young and old.

Needless to say it worked.

So I start this thread in the hope that the same mojo will work for the White Sox.

So, White Sox, win it for Bill in Oak Park, Steve in Wilmette, Irv in Rogers Park, who I have gone to so many games on 35th St with.

For the two guys that befriended me after a Good Friday afternoon game in April of 1981 when over 30,000 White Sox fans attended church on 35th St.

For John Kinsella, his son Ray and daughter-in-law Annie.

For Joe and Buck to ease their pain

For all the nameless White Sox fans I have met over the past 25 years. Go White Sox!

—**fenway**

Dedicated to . . . one of the best hitters in the history of the game: Frank Thomas.

—**Unregistered**

Dedicated to ...my grandpa Matthew Brown, who was a great fan and always cheered on the Sox. He passed away 14 years ago, but I know if hew were here right now he would be watching the games with me with a big smile on his face.

I believe in the 2005 Chicago White Sox because happiness is hanging out with the boys from 35th and Shields!

—swanson24

Dedicated to ...Ted "Double Duty" Radcliffe. Double Duty was a legendary star in the Negro Leagues and a frequent attendee at Sox games. He was always there for the games puffing on a big cigar. He passed away this August at the age of 103. I wish he could have seen this.

But for all the White Sox greats, living and deceased ... Nellie and Luis, Billy Pierce and Gerry Staley and Dick Allen and Luke Appling and the South Side Hitmen, the Winning Ugly Crew, and everyone who ever put on the uniform.

For Minnie Minoso. For Bill Veeck. For the Big Hurt.

And on and on and on ...

—The_Floridian

Dedicated to ...

For this whole run I just can't stop thinking about my dad and how I wish he were here right now. So for him ...

Chet
1921-1998
White Sox Fan

—michned

Dedicated to ...

I'll say do it for Chico.

—santo=dorf

Dedicated to ... PaleHoseGeorge, FarWestChicago, Daver, Voodochile, and rest of the WSI Moderator Staff, who have given us this wonderful place to talk about our Sox. Thanks, guys!

—RKMeibalane

Dedicated to . . .

Win it for your own damn selves.

And then with a little luck you can spend the rest of your life after baseball re-selling and re-telling the memory of your historic victory just like any number of members of the 1985 Bears team.

—ohnny bench

Dedicated to . . .

Win it for Johnny!

Win it for the whole damn White Sox Nation!!! We have been waiting a long time!

—bayzbol44

Dedicated to . . .

Win it for ME! I've been a fan for 30 years ...

Tonight it's all about ME!!

—MiamiSpartan

Dedicated to . . .

Win it for yourselves, but I would like them to win not for my enjoyment, but for my dad, who's been a fan since 1955. He became a Sox fan to tick off my aunt who was a Yankee fan. He later passed the disease on to me after I tried to deny it my first 14 years on the planet.

I'd love to pick up the phone tonight and have the voice on the other end, for once, not say, "God they f'ing suck!!"

Go Sox!!

—**Bobby Thigpen**

Dedicated to . . .

First and foremost, the Sox should win the pennant for themselves. They've scrapped, clawed, and worked like crazy to get to this position. Of course we fans will enjoy it, but they definitely deserve to enjoy this occasion.

They should also win this for...

… the fans who've believed in this team since day one.

... the people who've been suffering without a pennant since they were alive to see the "Go Go Sox" win in '59.

... the people like me who weren't alive back then, but can almost feel the same excitement and say, "So this was how it was back then?"

... the skeptics who believed this team wouldn't finish higher than 3rd in the division. Why? So the skeptics can choose their crow to be either original or extra crispy.

... the people who've constantly dissed the Sox, the fans, the ballpark, and the neighborhood nearby. Why? So all the Wrigley and Fenway lovers can see that it's not about an old ballpark or a trendy bar scene across the street, but a team that gives its all on the field where it counts the most

... and so on, and so on, and so on.

We've said since day one this team deserves respect. Now, the Sox are in a position where they'll get it and then some. Finish the job in Anaheim, Pale Hose!! Come home a pennant winner, and I'll guarantee you the turnout at Midway welcoming you back will be HUGE!!

Let's go, Go Go White Sox ... this fan, and millions of others, are proud of you!!

—hsnterprize

Dedicated to ...

As much as I hate to follow the trend (heck, that's why I'm a White Sox fan), I have to do what so many others have done and dedicate the 2005 championship to Grandpa. He convinced my mom to let me skip school back in 1990 for the last opening day at Old Comiskey Park. He drove me from Tampa to Sarasota to watch a spring training game in the late '80s. He sat through rain delays and double-headers. He passed away shortly after the Sox were eliminated in the 1993 ALCS, and I remember him saying, "We'll get 'em next year." Of course, the strike of '94 prevented that team from having a shot, but twelve years later, the '05 Sox finally did it. I'm sure Grandpa is smiling somewhere.

—**pudge**

Dedicated to . . .

Win it for all of us Sox fans who have been devoted for years! And for my dad and grandpa, who taught me to be a Sox fan!

—**naprvllesoxfan**

*Dedicated to . . .*my dad, who was there in '59 and who made me a Sox fan, and for my son, who I hope will be a Sox fan ...

—**joejacksonsdad**

*Dedicated to . . .*my father, who passed away 10 years ago. He was a lifelong fan who took me to my first game as a five-year-old kid. Even though my parents divorced when I was still young, my older brothers and I always wanted to take him one more time to a game, to kind of "heal old wounds." Well, that didn't happen, but this did, and I know he was watching. Rest in peace, James. The White Sox are champs.

—**RedHeadPaleHoser**

Dedicated to . . . Matthew Nicholas Riordan, the newest member of our family and my first nephew/godson. He joined us September 15 and has been a good luck charm since.

He's been a blessing in so many ways, and I had a picture of him in his White Sox cradle I made with the Sox blanket my mom made surrounded by hats, bibs, a pacifier, and a White Sox doll.

It sat there on top of my entertainment center the whole time.

I looked over to him and said, "Matty, we need something here."

And boy did we get it.

I have a bat with Willie Thompson and Carlton Fisk's autograph.

Willie was friends with my dad. And he got me a signed Fisk bat. Pudge wasn't much of an autograph guy.

For Willie to do that ... incredible.

I'm forever in his debt and I hope he knows what that meant to me.

—Hondo

Dedicated to . . .

Win tonight for my Dad who represents the loyal Sox fans that have been waiting since 1959.

Keep on winning for my daughter and all the Sox fans that will be too young to remember this magical summer.

GO SOX!!!

—**soxfan26**

Dedicated to . . . my father and our Sunday routine. Mass at Immaculate Conception. Breakfast at David's; McCuddy's would open at noon. Francine McCuddy for the first beer and pop of the day. Virginia would serve the hot dogs. The little guy servicing the back bar, a bat boy in the 30S, I think his name was Sharkey. Ronny the bookie with the great tier 4 seats. So many great Sox fans in the beer garden. Willie the peanut man. I love this team and I always will.

Thank you for the look on Katie's face when I woke her to tell her the magic number was now zero and that the Chicago White Sox were World Champions.

—**Gaelhound**

Dedicated to . . . **my dad, a** ten-year season ticket holder and a White Sox fan his whole life when his whole family besides him likes the team that plays on the North Side. He sold beer for the Cubs and White Sox in 1969 and watched the Cubs choke in front of him and has not been there since. Go White Sox.

—**chidavid18**

Dedicated to ...

> Win it for someone who's failing health may keep them from cheering on the White Sox for another year.
>
> Win it for the long-suffering fan who has known mostly misery during the baseball season and has the ulcers to prove it.
>
> Win it for the person who thought they raised their daughter right, only to see her marry a die-hard Cubs fan.
>
> Win it for the person who hates computers but goes to a baseball message board each day because they cannot get enough of the White Sox.
>
> Win it for all of the fans who gave up in anger and frustration only to come back because they just couldn't stay away.
>
> Win it for all of the White Sox fans everywhere who NEVER GAVE UP.
>
> Win it for the city of Chicago.
>
> Win it because the future is now and we may never pass this way again.
>
> Go White Sox ... Win or die trying ...
>
> **—harwar**

Dedicated to ...my uncle Steve, the biggest Sox fan I ever knew. He passed away on July 13, 2004. I miss him and can't help but think how excited he would be if he was still with us now ... GO SOX!

—**house215**

Dedicated to . . .the long-suffering Sox fans and the players who gave their all but fell short (i.e., Thomas, Hoyt, Burns, Fisk).

Also dedicated to the memories of Chico Caresquel and the "senor" himself, Al Lopez, who saw the team win their first WS in 88 years, then passed away four days later.

—**SOXSINCE'70**

Dedicated to . . .

Since the team is really a family, they are first off winning it for themselves. But surrounding the team is the support system, us fans, that pay their salaries, cheer them on, and defend the White Sox name to whoever will listen. So, White Sox, win it for all fans and players ever associated with Chicago's American League Ballclub.

—**veeter**

Dedicated to . . .

Now win this thing for the South Side, Chicago, yourselves, and long-suffering Sox fans everywhere.

—**goodsy72**

Dedicated to . . .all 1.75 million people who packed the city for the parade.

And to everyone too young to have heard those air raid sirens in '59.

—zach074

Dedicated to . . .George Burns. He was the young black guy; you'd see him at the park all the time, in his Sox hat and jersey, oh and in his wheelchair.

He was always a pleasure to talk to, and he never bitched about his fate. I always enjoyed the story he told me how he became a Sox fan.

He used to be a Cubs fan until they traded his favorite player, two-time batting champion Bill Madlock. Then the Cubs brought in an aging Bobby Murcer and gave him the same money Madlock was asking for, but Wrigley was denying!!

He switched over to the Sox and NEVER looked back. I wish George could've lived to see this!!

R.I.P., George; you'll never be forgotten! This one's for you.

—Wsoxmike59

Dedicated to . . .my dad, Dave Sr., who passed away February '04 at 50. This without a doubt would be a team he would be proud of to root for. I know he's up there with his dad, both with their Sox hats on cheering them on!

—pissonthecubs

Dedicated to . . .

> Just win it. I don't care who the hell for.

> **—illini81887**

*Dedicated to . . .*John Rooney!

> **—antitwins13**

*Dedicated to . . .*everyone at WSI, the greatest Sox fans I've ever met (even if it's just on the computer for now). You guys rox my Sox.

> "'Unless you people see miraculous signs and wonders,' Jesus told him, 'you will never believe'" (John 4:48).

> (Jesus commenting on Sox fans? Maybe ...)

> **—SweetnesSox**

Dedicated to . . .

> C'mon guys, win it for the Hawk.

> But especially, win it for my dad. He was just a kid in 1959 and has been a Sox fan ever since. Needless to say, he raised me right. (My sister though, is another story.)

> **—TheDarkGundam**

Dedicated to …my dad as well. He passed away six years ago, and he'll be the reason I shed tears when they win. There is no one I would have rather shared a celebratory beer and hug with. For you, Pops!

—chisox83

Dedicated to …

It's funny how 88 years can come and go without notice. Many of us thought we would never see a World Champion on the South Side. Many of us never did.

We still call him "The Old Man." He grew up a South Sider, 71st St. to be exact. He had many things going on in his young life, some not so pleasant. Raised by a single mother for a time, moved to Texas and back all before the age of 16. He was a White Sox fan. Born in 1936, he saw some horrible baseball teams, all the while staying faithful to the Sox.

Life eventually took him to Calumet City, to start a family. Deciding to live the American dream, he took his wife and two boys to Lansing, built a house there. In '69 he added two more boys to the roster. Before you could blink an eye, 1974 had rolled around. He moved his family to Indiana to avoid the property taxes of Cook County. What did he bring with? Four more Sox fans.

My earliest memories of the Sox begin around 1974, the red uniforms, Wilbur Wood and Bucky Dent. It was always "Go Sox" in our house, nothing else. Baseball season was six months of heaven, the smell of freshly cut grass, the "pop" of a fastball in that old Rawlings glove. A great time to be a kid.

In March of 1977, "The Old Man" passed, leaving a young family in some dire times. No real fault of his; he just worked way too hard, putting his family before his own health. He died just a few weeks before one of the most fun years in recent Sox fan memory. He never saw the South Side Hitmen. What fun he would have had that summer.

The White Sox had minor success in the years to follow. Winning Ugly in '83, 1993's Good Guys, the overachieving 2000 team. Knowing him, he would've had fun with us cheering for these teams that were doomed, hoping and praying from the bottom of his heart that each of these was "The Year."

As the 2005 season progressed, as the momentum built, I had but one person in mind. As the wins added up, something told me this was the year, the year the Sox would win it all for my dad. I was right. Finally.

Of course I hope they repeat, again and again. But if they don't win it all right away, the years between 2015 and 2020 would make a nice fit. You see, my kids will be able to remember clearly what a Sox championship meant to me, something I wasn't able to do for my dad.

This one's for you Old Man.
I cheered for you.
I cried for you.
I hugged my kids for you.
Good Guys Wear Black!

—**LuvSox**

Dedicated to . . . Bill Veeck.

> Wherever he is, I'm sure he's smiling that HUGE grin of his and drinking an appropriate beverage!
>
> **—IotaNet**

Dedicated to . . .

> I feel bad Frank Edward Thomas Jr. can't be a bigger part in this!
>
> This win is for him! Greatest player in White Sox history.
>
> **—Ron Karkovice**

Dedicated to . . . my grandpa, who took me to my first game!

> This one's for you.
>
> **—ShoelessJoeS**

Dedicated to . . . George Burns!!

> The biggest die-hard fan ever! Period.
>
> Wish he could be here to see this!!
>
> Go Sox!
>
> 2005 American League Pennant!!
>
> **—gosox83**

Dedicated to . . .my brother Jimmy, my mom, and her ancestors (and sorry for being so selfish, but ME!!!!).

And also John Cusack.

—**CJLove23**

Dedicated to . . .each and every one of us, and our loved ones, who have cheered, cried, sweat, bled, lived, and died by our beloved White Sox for all these years.

—**ChiSoxPatF**

Dedicated to . . .Grampy, thanks.

To Uncle Rich, okay they didn't re-sign Big Klu, but they finally got back to the Series.

—**Dancin' Homer**

Dedicated to . . .

Win it for me just because I'm a selfish bastard ...

Seriously, I found the White Sox almost completely on my own. For whatever reason I never had a friend or family member that introduced me to them on TV or radio or took me to my first game where I fell in love with them. I just loved the game of baseball and they are the team I started following.

I guess I have to give credit to my best friend. A Cubs fan.

We used to play baseball on my old NES, and he would always choose to be the Cubs. Well, since I also wanted to stay loyal to my home state, I always choose the Sox. The rest, as they say, is history ...

So as strange as it sounds: Win it for my friend, the Cubs fan. 'Cause without him I wouldn't be where I am today.

—Iwritecode

Dedicated to ...

Win it for the 1959 team.

Win it for all the teams that couldn't advance: 1983, 1993, 2000.

Win it for all the great teams that fell short: 1964, 1977, 1994, etc.

Win it for all the older fans who watched Mickey Mantle and Whitey Ford break their hearts and end their dreams year after year.

Win it for Minnie.

In Kenny We Trust

—TheOldRoman

Dedicated to ... Alex and Ursula Snelius ... I think she made a deal with the Good Lord.

—Musoxfan

Dedicated to . . .my uncle who was a die-hard Sox fan; wish that he was around to see it.

To my nephew who's currently serving our country in Iraq.

—silhouette

Dedicated to . . .my grandfather, who emigrated from County Cork, Ireland, to the South Side of Chicago in I think about 1913. He never learned to drive a car, but he did learn to love the Chicago White Sox. I thank him and those of his generation who handed down their rabid and unrepentant love for the White Sox (and hatred of the Chicago Cubs—it's part of the tradition), and remember him especially during this magical season.

To my dad for preserving this tradition by taking me to so many White Sox games when I was growing up despite the long trek—both geographically and culturally—from the Bulls/Bears/Cubs miasma of the northwest suburbs, and for never ever taking me to see a game at Wrigley Field.

I also think especially of Bill Veeck, who kept our White Sox in Chicago when they were on the verge of being moved to Florida or Colorado.

—Sox&Springsteen

Dedicated to . . .Grandpa. Sitting around, listening to games on his transistor radio with him put the White Sox in my blood. I'm sure he's up there somewhere, wearing his 1917 cap, rooting the boys on.

—Over By There

Dedicated to . . . my grandfather, who despite a rough childhood, managed to find a place in his heart for baseball and the White Sox. He then passed his love of the game and the Sox on to his son, who in turn passed his love of baseball and the Sox on to me.

I'm thankful that my dad was one of the first people I was able to high-five and hug after the Sox won it all. He was the one who took me to games when I was a kid, starting with a Sox-Milwaukee contest in 1974. I'm grateful that I'm able to still go to Sox games with him 31 years later and converse with him about a subject that has a great deal of meaning to both of us. And thanks, Dad, for teaching me math by using baseball stats (the batting average of Ed Herrmann plus the ERA of Wilbur Wood equals ...) and for going with me on those Interlake-Straight-A ticket days to watch the Sox play Texas and Cleveland. And thanks for being able to watch Game 7 with you.

Thank you. Thank you. Thank you.

Thanks, Grandpa Walsh, and thanks, Dad. Go Sox!!!!!

—MeteorsSox4367

Dedicated to ... **Hope**.

The season is for my Dad, Carmelo. He would have loved watching this team because of the way they played. I wish he would have been here to share this with us. My brother, my niece and nephew, and I learned to love sports. He taught us how to play the game, and this team plays the way he would have loved to see it played.

I hope that the White Sox win the Series, so I could remember Dad like I do now.

WIN OR DIE TRYING!

It's not just a marketing slogan; it's a lifestyle.

Dad would agree.

—archangelgabe66

Dedicated to ... my brother, who would be here watching the game with my dad and I except he is awaiting military deployment ... Let's send my brother overseas with a WHITE SOX WORLD SERIES WINNER!!

—SALUKIS15

Dedicated to ... all the generations of SOX fans come and gone ...

including my great uncles John and Steve who used to live in Whiting, IN.

This one's for you fellas ...

—Sad

Dedicated to ...my dad (passed away two weeks ago), who told me his story of a day at school when the Yankees and the Cubs were the two big teams in SE Wisconsin in the mid-40s. (Cubs were the closest geographically; the Yankees got a lot of players from Wisconsin schools—the Braves didn't move there for a few more years.) A sixth grader was in charge of the water fountain and would ask each kid, "Yankees or Cubs?" If you said "Yankees," you got a drink; if you said "Cubs" (like my dad's friend did before him), you got turned away.

Dad would be next and say "Yankees" and get his drink. He'd wipe the water off his face turn and correct himself, "I meant White Sox!"

I like that story.

This is for my dad and everybody like him—all the guys who worked long hours at American Motors and the steel mills, who busted their butts to put food on the table, a roof over your head, and tried to give people like me a better life, yet took the time to take it easy and take the family to the old park. (My dad never saw a game in the new park; didn't have the energy to go.)

This is for my mom, who took me to get Bill Melton's autograph 10 years ago and was singing the Chevrolet commercial he did and saw him light up and turn red that somebody remembered that cold morning with Pat Kelly, showering and singing. (I posed as some guy named "Frank" so the lady behind me could get her son an autograph.) Sixty years old now, I flash back to seeing her in that 1983 Sox visor and carrying around a seat cushion all the time.

This is for my 6-year-old daughter and 4-year-old son, who get to see how baseball is supposed to be played to win at any situation.

This is for my brother and I, who would fight over who got to be Ron Kittle in our Home Run Derby game. (I usually backed down and played as Greg Luzinski or Carlton Fisk to keep him quiet.)

But above all else, this is for everybody.

—VenturaSoxFan23

Dedicated to . . .my grandfathers—I wish they could have lived to see this. Thank God they laid down the law in our families and chose the Sox instead of the Cubs! And for my dad, who has talked baseball with me ever since I can remember! I can't wait to go to Game 2 with him!!! And for my kids, who've been attending games as long as they can remember—they deserve a winning start to their fandom.

—Lisa

Dedicated to . . .my departed father, many years ago, and to my children: one a teenager who is very excited, the other a six-month-old who watched many games and highlights this year cuddling with her daddy under the White Sox blanket. For all the beloved Sox players of the past who were not fortunate enough to feel this excitement. For Joe Jackson, for Frank Thomas, for us, the truly blessed.

—COOLPAPA

*Dedicated to . . .*my grandpa, Allen Dickson, a lifelong Sox fan and one of the greatest human beings to ever walk this earth ... Unfortunately he died a couple years back to an extremely rare liver disease that only 1 out of 300,000 cases to get it are male.

My most precious memories of him are watching Sox games with him on TV and going out to the back yard playing catch or hitting ... If it wasn't for him, I wouldn't be a Sox fan, nor love this sport as much as I do. Now I'm heading into my third year as a high school baseball assistant/pitching coach, although I have cerebral palsy.

Though he isn't here to witness what he waited all his life for, I'm sure he's up in heaven celebrating like crazy.

All this joy and happiness is dedicated to my Grandpa. I miss him and wish he was here to share this with …

Who do you dedicate this championship to?

—tadscout

*Dedicated to . . .*my grandpa and great grandpa. I never got the privilege of know either man, but I have no doubt that they are celebrating this glorious win together right now.

My great grandpa was Red Faber's cousin and they played baseball together. My grandpa told my mom that his father taught everything he knew, including how to throw his renowned spitball. He may have been exaggerating, hell, he probably was. But I know for a fact that those two would've loved to watch this year's team, and I would've been honored to watch it with them.

WORLD CHAMPIONS!

—**IA_soxfan**

Dedicated to . . .my grandfather Gilbert who lived in Chicago Heights as a die-hard Sox fan listening to games on his transistor radio, never getting to see a day like we just witnessed today. I never had the opportunity to meet him, but he is the reason my father and uncle are Sox fans, and thusly they passed it down to me. This championship is for you and my grandmother.

—**Foulke You**

Dedicated to . . .my grandpa Fred. He was the only other member of my family who is a die-hard sports fan. My mom keeps telling me about how excited he was in 1959 and how she even at 5 years old remembers Nellie and the rest of the team.

—**Soxfan35**

Dedicated to . . .my grandfathers and uncles who made us root for the true Chicago team—the South Side Irish White Sox!! They are resting in peace ... and having a few cold ones tonight!

—havelj

Dedicated to . . .my grandpa who played for the White Sox in their farm system in the '40s, who has waited his whole life for this and finally gets to see it.

—White_Sock

Dedicated to . . .the loyal and die-hard Sox fans in the evening of their lives. You have waited long for this. Enjoy it and be there when the flag is raised on opening day to see your dream come true.

—The Wall

Dedicated to . . .my father. He may have passed away this past July, but he always imbued me with a love of sports. I learned that from him. He was a die-hard sports fan, and although he wasn't a huge fan of either Chicago team, he let me make the decision myself. I chose the Sox, but it was he who brought me to my first Sox game, my first Cubs game, my first Cards game, my first playoff games in 1993 and 2000, and obviously oh so much more.

Dad, this one's for you. Too bad you couldn't have lived three more months to see this.

—Dspivack

Dedicated to . . .my aunt Tonia. She took me to my first Sox game when I was 9 years old.

She would be loving this moment.

—vegyrex

Dedicated to . . .all of us fans who stayed true to our Sox, who NEVER wavered or doubted this team was built for this very moment; to those who stood fearless in the face of the multitudes of Dark Clouds in September and said "Bah! We will be playing when it really counts!" and believed it!

And to all of the Morons and Mediots and Dark Clouds and Wussies: We fart in your general direction!

—Fuller_Schettman

Dedicated to . . .

October 26, 2005. 32,153 days have passed since Red Faber went the distance to beat the New York Giants in Game 6 of the 1917 World Series. My grandfather's eyes saw so much history, from the stock market crash to WWII to man's first steps on the moon ... but he never saw his favorite team win the World Series. This is for you, Grandpa. I'll see you soon at River Hills, with a shot of blackberry brandy ... trying to fight the tears back.

—Erik The Red

Dedicated to …my grandpa Ken, who passed away in 1998. I'll be going down to Mount Greenwood to put a Sox flag on his grave this weekend.

—Hendu

Dedicated to …my beloved wife. We first met and fell in love in South Side Chicago. Attending three of the White Sox opening days (2000-2002), seeing the excitement of 2000 season together, and watching this year's incredible run together. My memory of the White Sox would never be complete without you. I love you, BB.

—ferdinandshen

Dedicated to …anyone who paid to see this franchise back in 1918 through today. Whether you're a grandparent with 50 grandchildren or the guy sitting at the corner wearing an authentic ripped-up 1990 White Sox shirt with a sign "will work for food." Basically anyone who gave a damn about the franchise that supposedly had no fans or appeal. Especially for those of you overseas or killed in action, you're the ones making the ultimate sacrifice so these ball players can make your dream come through. For that I dedicate this win to all of us, and thank all of you; we may have moments of disagreement or fighting, but we are a big ole family of brothers and sisters and I love each and every one you.

—getonbckthr

54

Dedicated to . . . my dad, who was a lifelong Sox fan and in the 85 years he lived only saw the Sox in the '59 series. My last memory of him is watching the Sox game together the day before he died this last June. We will be decorating his grave this weekend with World Champion White Sox flags. I know he's enjoying tonight in heaven with all the dearly departed White Sox fans. I wish I could have celebrated with him.

—springrovesoxfan

Dedicated to . . . every Sox fan from the beginning that has kept this team here in Chicago to the fans of now that continue the South Side Pride.

To my mom and older brother for being the Sox fans in the family growing up and taking me to the games as a kid.

And of course to my girl ... for sitting out in the cold with me every year waiting for tickets to go on sale, sitting through those cold April/September games and being with me at every game over our last four years ...

We are the 2005 Champions

Thank you, White Sox ... 2005 WORLD SERIES CHAMPIONS

—Chicago

Dedicated to . . . every real Sox fan that ever stepped foot on this earth.

My dad, who taught me all I know about the White Sox from ages 0-15, and who actually took back a Cubs pajama set given to me by my aunt for the hospital claiming, "He's not wearing this; he's a Sox baby." After that my dad slipped on my White Sox pajama-jersey pajamas.

And also to my grandfather, the late/great Rich "The Rock" Kraetsch. A man who I've never been able to see, never been able to talk to, never been able to give a handshake to, yet I have taken his name and his legacy as a caring man and a devout White Sox fan, a trait he passed to my father and that I will pass on to my children. All I can say is, "Rock," I hope you're celebrating up there or wherever you may be; you're definitely in my heart.

—FedEx227

Dedicated to ...Robin Ventura, who turned me from an 11-year-old kid from the northwest suburbs who didn't know any better to a lifelong Sox fan in 1991.

To the '91 playoffs with the Braves over the Pirates in 7, and the Twins over the Braves in 7 in the greatest Series ever, that turned me into a lifelong baseball fan.

And finally to my dad, from the cornfields of southwest Iowa, who never had a baseball team, but adopted the Sox to support me, and died in February of this year, just over eight months short of seeing my dreams come true ...

I know I cheated by having three, but anyone else want to join in?

—Disantinon

Dedicated to . . .my dad, the greatest guy I have ever known.

—ASUSOXGRL

Dedicated to . . .my grandpa and dad. My 84-year-old grandpa was just weeks ago diagnosed with terminal cancer and has but months to live. Just as I called my dad and cried after the third out, he called his dad and did the same. Some people have no idea just how big of a day this was in my family's life. But everyone here does. Twenty-five or thirty guys down in Houston tonight made an old, sick man very, very happy tonight.

—ilsox7

Dedicated to . . .my mom. For dragging me around to Marquette Boys Baseball games. For making me get perfect attendance and good grades in grammar school so I received those straight A and perfect attendance vouchers for free Sox tickets. It all boils down to her. She doesn't appreciate this title as I do, but she also has no idea how she influenced my love for the game.

I will let her know this morning.

—David Tamosaitis

Dedicated to . . . my dad, the most important person in my life.

> To my grandfather (R.I.P.) who made us all Sox fans.
>
> To Bill Veeck, my favorite pic is of me, my granddad, and him.

—fozzy

Dedicated to . . . Frank Thomas, a truly great player and a truly great cheerleader during the playoffs and to all the Chicago White Sox TRUE fans, dead or alive.

—henchmanUK

Dedicated to . . . Superstar Lamar Johnson. Hit it here.

—34 Inch Stick

Dedicated to . . . my dad, who took me to my first Sox game back when I was six.

> We struggled through some ugly baseball games (and uniforms) over the years, and had our hearts broken on more than a couple of occasions with the Hitmen and the '83 team that got pounded by the Orioles and the '94 team that never got the chance.
>
> I only wish that he were here to see it. But I suspect he had a pretty good view from up there.
>
> Thanks, Dad!

—Bucky F. Dent

Dedicated to . . .my dad. We've went to numerous Sox games together, and he got me into the Sox when I was young. I'm glad I got to share this win with my dad and that he got to see it in his lifetime.

—MsSoxVixen22

Dedicated to . . .my aunt Marycolette, who died yesterday. It was something we knew was coming, and my mom and sister were on their way to her home in Tennessee when she died.

—Railsplitter

Dedicated to . . .my late brother-in-law, who despite being raised in a family of lil' bear fans became a die-hard SOX fan. He died when he was 17. I got a little teary-eyed last night when I thought of how much he would have loved this.

For you, Tim!

—Church Turtle

Dedicated to . . .

Win it for me!

—DenverSock

Dedicated to . . .my dad. He died in 1994, with his last experience on earth as a Sox fan shattered by that strike.

59

We grew up in central Illinois, where Sox fans were few and far between. We went to as many games as we could though. My dad taught us to be proud of the fact that we were Sox fans and to ignore the taunts and derision of the multitudes of Cubs and Cardinal (admittedly though, the Cards were our second favorite team after the Sox) fans that were all around us ... many of whom didn't even acknowledge that the city of Chicago had an American League franchise.

My brother back home called me this morning and told me that he is going to purchase a Sox World Champion cap and lay it on his grave marker. I just hope it matches the one he's wearing right now up in heaven.

—BedfordChisox

Dedicated to . . . my dad, who started taking my brother and me to Sox games when we were very young, even though he's a Cubs fan.

—asindc

Dedicated to . . . my dad. I watched many games with him growing up, and I was able to watch a World Series win with him. I feel lucky.

—#1venturafan

Dedicated to ...

This was even better than when Scott Skiles led good ol' Plymouth High School to the '82 Indiana State Basketball Championship. Dad got to see that one.

To my dear departed Dad, ol' alibi Ike, and to Colonel Scott A Tackett, Sat46. Now they can rest in peace.

—bench

Dedicated to ... my dad, who took me to my first game in April of 1978 when I was five. He left us in November of 1990. He would have been so happy today.

—Greg1983

Dedicated to ... all the older Sox fans (50+) who have suffered much longer than the 23 years I've been on this earth and for all those Sox fans who passed without seeing the South Side win a title.

This for Joe Crede for having the month of his life, and the rest of the team at that.

Here's to Uribe for showing me up with his leather when I've cursed him at the plate.

Can't forget my dad, who introduced me to the beautiful game of baseball.

Here's to you Sox fans! You deserve it!

—JOECREDEFAN

Dedicated to . . . me, the Sox fans in my family, and to all of the players that have made their home on the South Side and never had the chance to experience of winning a World Series.

Now when the flub fans start with us again, we have the ultimate comeback, "Hey, what did your team do this October?"

—**Stroker Ace**

Dedicated to . . . my grandfather, who instilled the love of baseball in me.

To my buddy Russell, who instilled the love of the Sox in me.

—**whitesoxwilkes**

Dedicated to . . .

My hubby, Hendu, who's the reason I'm a White Sox and baseball fan.

His dad for waiting so long.

His grandpa, who's no longer here, but who hopefully is celebrating somewhere in another space.

Frank Thomas and Jerry Reinsdorf, the whole White Sox organization, and all the die-hard fans.

—**Mrs. Hendu**

Dedicated to . . .my dad, who passed away in 1977 when I was 11 years old.

> In the short time I had with him he taught me everything about baseball. Hours and hours we sat watching the Sox and going to Comiskey Park.
>
> He took me to my first game. It was opening day 1971 against the Twins. Sox won with a run in the bottom of the ninth, and I remember being lifted high above my dad's head in celebration.
>
> I remember hearing the stories about the '59 team. He would say, "Luis and Nellie! The greatest double play combo I have ever seen!"
>
> I now share those memories and passion with my kids. My 10-year-old son, David, was named after my dad. We shared this title together at the United Center last night with 5,000 other Sox fans.
>
> So here's to you, Dad.
>
> Thank you for raising me a Sox fan.
>
> **—Special Ed**

Dedicated to . . .

> **Set to the tune of Bob Dylan's "Song to Woody":**
> We swept them 1,000 miles from the Cell
> Our pitching and defense gave all of them hell
> Our hitters got on and over and in
> That's how we got the 2005 World Series win
>
> Hey all you South Siders, I wrote you this tune

The ticker tape parade will be happening soon
Been a long time since we let out such a cheer
Now grab your glass and raise up your beer

Here's to Minnie and Nellie and Little Looie too
And to all of the grinders who played ball with you
Here's to Harold, Pudge, Robin, Frank, and the rest
Your White Sox team is finally the best

Let's toast to the fans who won't "stop believing"
And to 88 years of misery leaving
Now I've got just one more toast to say
To all the other great fans who didn't live to see this
day

—maurice

Dedicated to . . .the memory of all the Sox fans who didn't live to see
their team win a World Series.

And to Shoeless Joe and Buck Weaver and everyone
else who didn't deserve to be treated the way they
were after the 1919 World Series.

This was for them.

—graham5

Dedicated to . . .my dad, who took me to my first Sox game at age three
in 1969. He instilled the love of baseball and the Sox
in me that will always live on. Even though he passed
away in 1978, he's looking down and smiling today.

To all the other Sox faithful that have passed on without seeing this wonderful day, especially Bill Veeck, Shoeless Joe, Harry Caray, and Andy (the Clown) Rozdilsky. There's no need to be bitter anymore.

—russ99

Dedicated to . . . my dad, born in 1911, died in 1999. Grew up on Leavitt near what is now UIC. Was old enough to remember the 1919 team, and he swore the aftermath of that is what turned him into a die-hard. Couldn't help rooting for the underdog, all through the '20s, the '30s, the '40s, the '50s, the '60s, the '70s, the '80s, and the '90s. The '94 season was the last that he managed to follow; after that, Alzheimer's prevented him from keeping tabs on the team. The strike made me bitter for a while, I'll admit, because it cancelled any chance he'd see a Series championship.

Now, going to the game with my kids makes us feel connected to my dad. I'm not a mystical person, but I do feel his presence at the park, even though he saw 99 percent of his games across the street at Old Comiskey. So I sure hope you all are right, that departed ones will see a championship at last.

Here's one for Jean Shepherd, too.

My dad in the Sox hall of fame, 1991.

My dad on the concourse at New Comiskey
Park, with partially demolished old park
in the background.

—Vernam

Dedicated to ...my **dad in Heaven!!**

My dad past away in January of 1998, and when I was at Game 2 of the ALCS when the count was 0-2 on Crede, I looked up at the sky and said, "Dad, we need your help right now." Well, the rest is history, and today the Sox are the 2005 champions. During the last out, I looked at my mom and dad's picture (my mom passed this past January) and said, "I know you're both smiling!"

This ranks up with the birth of my kids. I just don't know what else to say except I LOVE BEING A SOX FAN and will cherish this moment forever!!

—barryball

Dedicated to ...my grandfather on my dad's side. He was really an overall Chicago sports enthusiast ... He took my dad when he was two weeks old to the stadium for his first Hawks game in 1948, and to many Sox games at the Old Comiskey. He died in 1998. I know my grandfather rooted for the Cubs, but it was an unwritten rule that when it came down to the Cubs vs. the Sox, our family rooted White Sox.

And to my dad, who took me to my first Sox game at the Old Comiskey (I can't even remember the day, or who won ... but it was against the Kansas City Royals, and I do remember seeing George Brett). My dad died in 2001 to a rare form of bone marrow cancer. He was only eleven in 1959, so I can only imagine what he would have thought about seeing the White Sox get past the ALDS.

I distinctly remember him telling me in '93, "I never thought I'd see champagne on a Sox uniform again." Really puts this season into perspective for me ... My dad lived fifty-three years and saw four champagne-soaked uniforms. Sox fans, we tied that in the course of about one month this year!!

—supertwangreverb

Dedicated to . . .

I'm a first generation White Sox fan, so this goes to everyone that has been waiting longer than my 18 years of age.

—kevingrt

Dedicated to . . . my dad, who took me to my first Sox game in 1944.

He never deserted them, no matter how tough things got.

He taught me what it was to be a fan and to not turn my back on my team.

My dad would have had tears in his eyes had he been lucky enough to see this.

He passed away in 1970.

Thanks, Dad.

This one's for you.

—CHEESESOXER

Dedicated to . . . **Romanzz**

My father would have loved this team. Hardworking, unselfish, and good humored, they never quit when things looked darkest. They knew what they had to do and did it.

My dad took me to my first Sox game when I was six, forty years ago. It was the first of many. As my own children grew up, he was always taking them to games, including every home opener. He loved the Sox, and he loved that I loved them too.

I know he was up there cheering them on.

This one is for you!

Go Sox!!

—Reminds me of 83

Dedicated to . . . my dad, who is a lifelong Sox fan, and we had planned to go to the All-Star game until he got sick.

Fortunately, he's better now, and he has lived long enough to see our team win the World Series.

Thanks, Dad! Thank you, White Sox!

—miker

Dedicated to . . . **Ozzie, not the manager.**

Had I seen this prior to the start of the season I would have posted the following:

Win it for Ozzie, a former Cuban League broadcast announcer who we met while going to and from Sox games in '99 on the red line. He had season tickets on the third base side and always listened to the radio broadcast while sitting in his seats, no doubt reliving a part of his former life. This elderly man whom I had never would have met took the time, the night I caught a Brooke Fordyce home run ball, to record all the sports broadcasts on TV (English and Spanish stations) and make a highlight reel of my catch which he gave to me the next game. To me, he is and will always be the definition of a Sox fan. God bless him wherever he may be now.

—denev1

Dedicated to . . . **us and the REAL HEROES the Sox players.**

This is to all of us who have been made fun of, laughed at for being a Sox fan. I don't think we are second class anything. Today we should be and will be FIRST CLASS because we as a whole except for few dumb butts rooted through the good and the bad and stood by our men. I know this has been the time of my life, and I still can't stop crying.

—nash316yo

Dedicated to . . . my grandma, who died this past August. She never got to see Chicago win a World Series in all her years, but I know she's smiling in Heaven right now and probably having a few cold ones. Also to anyone who has ever been a Sox fan. Our wait is finally over!

—jcirish85

Dedicated to . . .my dad, lifelong Cubs fan who didn't get to experience what his daughter is experiencing today. My dad was such a role model for sportsmanship and would watch Sox games with me and be genuinely happy for me when they won. It wouldn't surprise me one bit if he prefers this over a Cubs championship just to make his little girl happy. That's the kind of person he was.

Miss you, Dad ... but my White Sox did it!!

—LongLiveFisk

Dedicated to . . .my brother Dave, who loved the Sox dearly. He died of cancer in 1999. I wish he could have seen this.

—RhubarbStew

Dedicated to . . .my grandfather, whom I never met, but who became the first of what is now four generations of die-hard Sox fans.

He was heartbroken in '59, but I'm sure he is smiling now, looking down on this great season.

Thank you, White Sox!

—jayc

Dedicated to . . .my grandfather, who was everything a Sox fan symbolized. He grew up on the South Side and hated everything North Side, a Sox fan and Chicago Cardinals fan. When he and my dad lived in Downer's Grove, he took the train every morning to his job at a factory. He was born in 1919 and died in 1999. He was the first one I thought about when the boys were mobbing each other at the mound.

To my great uncle, Bernie, who played minor league baseball with the White Sox. He also wasn't able to live long enough to see this, but I'm sure he saw it from where he is now.

Also to my cousin, Mike, who died at age 24 of a brain tumor. He was a Sox fan until his last breath.

All three of these guys gave the Sox a little help this week.

—**ndu3t4**

Dedicated to ...my grandfather who passed a couple years ago and my great grandfather who first found the connection with the Sox, despite living on the North Side. I would also like to dedicate this to my wonderful grandfather who in is the hospital right now and to my dad for taking me to Game 1 of the World Series. I'll never forget it!!

—**NowBatting19**

Dedicated to ...**my dad.**

Even though he grew up in a Cubbie household, he's a die-hard fan. He took me to my first game when I was two, bought me an autographed Frank Thomas rookie card when I was in first grade, and I've been hooked ever since. He was the first person I talked to after the final out. I'm so happy he got to see this. Thanks, White Sox!

—Hoffdaddydmb

Dedicated to . . .my sons, Brad (aka Santo=Dorf) and Jack, who have allowed me to share with them a great love for the team of my youth.

To my dad and his friend the late Bill Veeck, who showed me joy in simply living.

To each and every one of you, my fellow travelers on the road to the pennant.

Again the magic number is 162, but never before have I been able to say that with the confidence and joy as I do today.

—JACK

Dedicated to . . .my great Aunt Sophie, who raised both me and my dad on White Sox baseball from 35th and Damen.

—bestkosher

Dedicated to . . .my dad, who made me a Sox fan from birth. He lived through all the heartbreaks. After the strike, he was convinced that that '94 was the year for the Sox and was away from the team for a few years. It took me, his son, and my enthusiasm to bring him back several years later to the team he loved his whole life. Unfor-

73

tunately he passed away in May, but I know he was watching from above, and maybe helping the boys a little bit.

—pauliemvp

Dedicated to . . .my dad, for taking me to my first game at Comiskey. Thanks for putting me on the path towards something that's generated so much sweet sorrow and even more joy, for being there to share each postseason win with either in person or on the phone.

To my college roommates for taking a casual fan and turning him into a raving lunatic.

To all my WSI friends and family for sharing in the emotion that is a passion for this team, over the years, through the season, and through this magical postseason. Especially thanks to PHG, Daver, VC, West, VC, and the rest of the mods for providing this amazing place for Sox fans.

To Jerry Reinsdorf, Kenny Williams, and Ozzie Guillen for making this all possible.

To Frank Thomas, the greatest player in team history, and to this fan, the greatest in MLB history. Always a class act to the fans, always respected the game, and always represented the game, team, and city better than I could have hoped, despite media portrayals to the contrary.

To the whole team for being a group not only that brought this title home, but for being a group that we as fans could be especially proud of for your character, hard work, and team-first attitude.

And most of all, to my wife and kids for being there to share this moment, for putting up with my neurotics during games, for sharing so many special moments at the park during the season, and making the memories of this title truly special.

Thank you all.

—Flight #24

Dedicated to . . .my grandfather, who died in 1990, and my uncle, who died five years later. Both were avid Sox fans. I know they're both looking down and smiling right now.

—spawn

Dedicated to . . .my parents, the reason I am a Sox fan ... never even thought of taking me to a Cubs game growing up.

—SouthsideFathead

Dedicated to . . .my beautiful wife, thanks for loving me, and supporting my love for the WORLD SERIES CHAMPIONS CHICAGO WHITE SOX!

To my brothers: the countless games, memories, tears of frustration, arguments, and now tears of joy. If we had to, we would do it all over again. We bleed Sox Pride and will do so forever ...

To the Chicago White Sox, ALL of you, THANK YOU!

—Rocky Soprano

Dedicated to ...my dad, who thankfully raised me a Sox fan and who busted his butt as a machinist all his life so I could go to school and not have to work in a hot sweaty shop. Now I work and live in a whole other world though I'll never forget where I came from. Thanks, Pop!

—haganaga

Dedicated to ...all my grandparents, but especially my two grandmothers, one of whom I know was a Cubs fan, but that's okay; she'd be happy anyway.

To my family, most of whom I converted to Sox fans.

Lastly, to my three-year-old son, who's almost as big a Sox fan as I am. Such a smart boy.

—Iron Dragon

Dedicated to ...my grandparents. They were both Cubs fans but took me to my first Sox game 18 years ago and I was instantly taken in by the team.

To my girlfriend, who roots for my "Go Go Sox" with me, even if she's a Cubs fan at heart.

To my roommate, who kept my nerves from frying completely when the Sox were losing the division lead like it was out of style.

To Kenny, Oz, Coop, Walker, Raines, Cora, and so on. Terrific job with these players.

To the players themselves, thank you!

—Dan Mega

Dedicated to . . .my dad, who was born in 1917 and passed away in 1976. He wasn't a sports enthusiast, but he bought me my first transistor radio. I soon found the Sox and spent many 1960's weekends walking around the yard with that radio glued to my ear listening to Bob Elson and Red Rush. This means so much.

—GeauxSox

Dedicated to . . .my father for taking me to my first game and letting me take off of school every year to go to opening day. I'm glad we were able to enjoy this World Series together.

To my mom for letting my dad take me out of school to go to ball games, for buying me Sox shirts and hats and coming to the games with us.

—chisoxfan64

Dedicated to . . . all the Sox fans that have waited a very long time to see this or even the young ones; it is a great time in Sox history, something most people will never forget.

To my parents that got me tickets to playoff games and regular season games. Also, they bought many other Sox merchandise for me: hats, shirts, and other memorabilia.

To my girlfriend, who went with me to the games, despite not being a huge Sox fan and cheering them on with me and celebrating the Sox championship with me. Also, for being able to watch every game with me even when she didn't want to.

—Dansoxfan04

Dedicated to . . . my dad and my brother—it was the most amazing thing attending Game 2 with them! We did it, boys!

—Get Back There!

Dedicated to . . . my mother, Mary, who had the patience and time to take me to dozens of games as a child, thereby instilling in me a love for the White Sox.

—ThinWhiteDuque

Dedicated to . . . my father, who was not a baseball fan but took time to take me to see the White Sox play. You are my hero, and I am thankful for everything you've done for me.

To Brad, who took me to my very first game at Old Comiskey. It was a night that has been etched in memory forever ,and I hope that we can do it again someday.

To my friends, who have suffered through the years with me. The '80s, the '90s, the '00s, and now 2005. Finally!

To my wife, who has been willing to lend an ear whenever talking about the team and its history. You'll be a die-hard fan yet!

To my son, who I was able to watch the final three outs of the World Series with. I love you and I look forward to watching many more White Sox games with you.

And to all of the players, coaches, broadcasters, and personnel who have put their hearts on the line for the White Sox organization. You have given me many wonderful moments in my life—none better than 10-26-2005.

—nccwsfan

Dedicated to . . .my uncle for taking me to my first Sox game as a child. This is for every former Chicagoan that still has the city in their heart. This is for all the Pumas in Rensselaer that rooted this team on from day one!

—gregoriop

Dedicated to ...my father. He took me to my first game when I was barely old enough to walk. We live several time zones from each other and don't get to talk much. When we do, it's usually about the White Sox. When we won the World Series, I called him, and all I could say was, "Dad, we just won the World Series!" And all he could say was, "I know!" The Sox winning has taught me that what I thought was impossible actually is possible.

—Argalarga

Dedicated to ...my best friend Mindy that passed away before Game 1 of the Boston series. I swear she was out there looking out for me, and this is the greatest gift she's ever given me. Thank you, Mindy, and your nametag will rest around my neck for the rest of my life.

—Chrisaway

Dedicated to . . .my dad, who taught me the meaning of being a Sox fan and that we are the greatest fans in the world. He instilled a passion in me that will never die.

—PicktoCLick72

Dedicated to . . .the people who loved watching them play today and to those who will hear the stories that will be passed on for generations.

—comiskey2000

Dedicated to . . .my grandfather for being a Sox fan and seeing the World Champion White Sox of 1917. He must have been a big reason my dad was a Sox fan. He left us in 1980.

To my dad, who wasn't around yet in 1917. The story is told that Dad became so stressed while the Sox were trying to wrap up the American League pennant in '59 that he had to take the dog for a walk and wasn't entirely sure what to make of the ensuing air raid sirens. He took me to my first game in 1969 when I was seven. It was a White Sox winner over the Oakland A's, on a pinch hit home run by Pete Ward. Dad and I went to many games together over the years, including opening day every year, along with his dad while he was still here. He missed the 2005 World Champion Chicago White Sox by five years, and we miss him very much.

And finally to my son, who only had to wait 14 years for a White Sox World Championship. I hope it's the first of many more to come for all of us.

—ja1022

Dedicated to . . . Minnie Minoso, who belongs in the HOF, and to my dad, who when I said to him, "Will you take me to a game," said, "Today? Sure." 1952, Sox beat Boston 4-3, Sherm Lollar with a homer (they didn't call it a walk-off then), in the 9th.

Dad was a Cubs fan.

—minnieistheman

Dedicated to . . . those Sox fans living and dead who remained true for years upon years upon years.

It is also for those rare individuals who actually wore the colors but didn't get the chance to make the Series in Chicago, players like Hoyt Wilhelm, Joe Horlen, Gary Peters, Dick Allen, "Goose" Gossage, Tommy John, Ken Berry, Johnny Buzhardt, Scotty Fletcher, Oscar Gamble, Eric Soderholm, Wilbur Wood, Ron Hansen, Ed Herrmann, J.C. Martin, Ray Herbert, Juan Pizarro, Richie Zisk, Walt Williams, Ron Kittle, Jack McDowell, Robin Ventura, Chet Lemon, Greg Luzinski, Pete Ward, Ron Hansen, Donn Pall, and so many others who just didn't have the same good fortune as the 2005 club.

All of those who came before should be enjoying this moment.

—Lip Man 1

Dedicated to . . . my wife and kids, who made this season all the more enjoyable. This season would not have been anywhere near as fun if I was not able to share it with them.

—Fredsox

Dedicated to . . . all the Sox fans who rooted through the glory and gloom for their beloved Pale Hose. It was a long time coming ... But how oh sweet it is!!

This is also for the players who proudly wore the White Sox uniform on those chilly April openers through the dog days of sweltering heat of summer and those crisp days of fall, giving their all.

This one is for the guys at WSI who carried the torch to relight the fire when hopes were smoldering and others felt the heavens falling. Their knowledge of Sox baseball, with sage-filled scribe and oration, candidly perpetuates the greatness of the organization and informs the neophyte of Chicago White Sox baseball historical precedent. The guys know baseball ... more than I can say for some of the scribes scribblin' for the fish wraps peddled in town.

This one is for Chicago, a city whose fans have repeatedly climbed to the top of the mountain on so many occasions in the past only to fall from the precipice. Time to plant the flag on the summit and beat the chest. Second City no more to no one.

Lastly this is for Dad. He took the time to introduce me to this great pastime, took me to Comiskey amid all of you faithful die-hards, and solidified this love affair with my White Sox.

Big Klu says, "When you step in the box you go to war."

—**Big Klu 59**

Dedicated to . . . my late grandma, who used to take me to Old Comiskey Park when I was quite little. These were the acts that instilled a lifetime of loving baseball and the White Sox. Thanks, Grandma, that one was for you.

—**mjmcend**

Dedicated to . . . my father and mother, Mike and Dyana Silaggi, who raised me to cheer for the Good Guys.

To my brother, Jeffrey Silaggi, who made sure I always rooted for the Good Guys.

To my sister and brother-in-law, Erin and Jonathon Fries, thanks for taking me in when I had nowhere else to go and allowing me to enjoy this memorable season with people I love.

Thank you.

—**SOXintheBURGH**

Dedicated to . . . my dad, who took me to my first Sox game, sitting in the golden box seats behind the Sox dugout at the "Old" Comiskey Park in the early '80s when they used to cost $9.25 a ticket. He passed away on January 6, 1986, and never lived to see any of his favorite teams win a world championship. None would have been sweeter than this one.

To my grandpa, who told us stories of watching the Sox play in a "prairie," as he called it, before they built the "Old" Comiskey Park. He never went anywhere without his transistor radio so he could listen to the Sox games.

I know they're both up there celebrating now!

—Dolly

Dedicated to . . .Chico Carrasquel and the many other White Sox players and family that are no longer with us. Everyone living and dead share together this common bond we call the Chicago White Sox. We have these memories forever. Believe it.

—Black Sox

Dedicated to . . .my husband, who introduced me to the White Sox. He's been a fan since he was "in the womb" and has stood by this team through all of its ups and downs. As long as I have known him, his greatest wish in life was to see the White Sox win the World Series. Well, honey, believe it. This World Champion White Sox team is dedicated to you.

—gogochisox1917

Dedicated to ...my uncle George, who saved me from a life of Cubs fandom by taking me to the Old Comiskey Park when I was a child. He caught one of Luis Aparicio's rare home run balls on the bounce and handed it to me.

Man, I wish I knew what happened to that ball over the years.

Thanks, Uncle George, and I'm sorry you didn't get to see this moment.

And of course to all of the great players over the years who just didn't make it for one reason or another. The list is endless, and many messages have named most of them.

And lastly, to all of the great knowledgeable fans, who followed the Sox through thick and thin. Some of the best baseball people I've known, and never a bandwagon in sight.

—Blancos Medias

Dedicated to ...my mother, Dee, who passed away on June 4th this summer.

During our last conversation, she only wanted to talk about how happy I must be that the Sox were rolling along in first place and maybe this will be the season, never mentioning how sick she had gotten and the pain she was suffering. She was a great woman, and I know she went to heaven and helped push the Sox over the top.

She was a die-hard baseball fan who loved the Pirates (her buccos of the '60s and '70s) and later became a Cubs fan because she thought Harry Carey was the greatest. The kind of women she is however made her root for the Sox against the Cubs because one of her sons (me) was obsessed with the Sox.

I miss her dearly but know she was with me the night we won the Series.

—billyvsox

Dedicated to . . .my dad, Ed Miller, who has been waiting 56 years to see this moment. He took me to my first White Sox game about 10 years ago, and I've been a loyal fan ever since. Thanks, Dad!

—bringfrankback

Dedicated to . . .my father, who got me interested in baseball as a child, took me to my first professional games (both Sox and Cubs), enrolled me in Little League beginning in the first grade, and even coached and umpired our leagues as me and my brothers got older. He passed away almost exactly 10 years ago to the date the White Sox won the World Series—October 21, 1995. Without him, I don't know if I would have ended up having the same relationship I do have to the greatest sport ever played. Dad, even though you were more of an Indians fan having grown up in Ohio, this one's for you.

—cheeses_h_rice

Dedicated to . . . mom's parents and all my family and friends in Chicago. I'm a lifelong White Sox fan although its only 19 years, and I know they would of loved to see this. Plus for my mom who helped inspire me to be a White Sox fan. Also, to everyone in Chicago.

—Greg Bergman

Dedicated to . . . all the kids on the playground at Grace McWayne school in Batavia in 1959, when our hopes were high. In our innocence we didn't know that "next year" would turn into 46 years.

And to my son, who is carrying on the SOX torch. I am so proud of you.

—fisk4ever

Dedicated to . . . my dad and grandpa who took me to so many games as a kid that I can't remember. Every game I went to with my grandpa was cold, windy, rainy. Didn't matter what time of year. Being there for the first two home World Series games reminded of those days with him. Even if box seats aren't $5 anymore. I saw a White Sox winner for all three of us this week. And for my little nephew, too young to really understand what just happened. May he grow up with our same passion for the Sox. You can bet his uncle will have something to say about that!

—Desert Rat

Dedicated to . . .all the people in Chicago who for so long had to put of with the media crap and the negativity surrounding this team. After a World Series victory it doesn't matter what the media, Cubs fans, or anyone else says about you or the White Sox because of the 2005 World Series!

—Jerome

Dedicated to . . .my father. I was born and raised in Toronto but am one of the biggest Sox fans around. My father, who was a Blue Jays fan, still supported me and took me to see the Sox every time they came to Toronto. How much I would have loved to be with him when the Sox won the other night. I know you were looking down on me. Thanks, Dad!

—LuzinskiFan

Dedicated to . . .the fans that have been there all the way, plain and simple.

—NSSoxFan

Dedicated to . . .my great auntie Jo, who used to write letters constantly to the Sox telling them what was wrong and who to trade, believing that they would actually listen to her! And who until the day she died watched every game and kept score, even at home! I know she's smiling down right now!

—VenturaFan23

Dedicated to ...

> **Thanks, Dad, for starting the biggest addiction of my life ...** and the only healthy one!
>
> **—arbutron**

Dedicated to ... my grandfather who passed away this past August; he meant so much to my family and was a big Sox fan!!

> **—illini81887**

Dedicated to ... me dammit! Meeeee!

> **—joepoe**

Dedicated to ... **Dad.**

> My great grandfather came to Chicago from Wales in the early 1900s. He worked as a calligrapher in the steel mills and quickly became a Sox fan, celebrating in 1917 when the team won the Series. In the early '50s he started to take my father to see the Sox, and like many of his generation his boyhood heroes were Fox and Pierce and Aparacio and the rest of the Go Go Sox. My dad saw lots of great teams and lots of great players, but no championship. He died in 1984, months after the heartbreak of the Winning Ugly team.
>
> I was fortunate enough to see Game 4 in Houston, and as I was jumping up and down in ecstasy, I couldn't

help but think of my dad. He would have loved this team, and my only regret about this incredible season was that he wasn't here to enjoy it. So, Dad, we finally did it. The Sox are the champions, and I thank you for giving me the love of baseball and the Chicago White Sox.

—Craig Reed

Dedicated to . . .my grandfather who started it all. It's also dedicated to my friend Julius, who passed away a few weeks ago.

—CubsfansareDRUNK

Dedicated to . . .

With the White Sox winning their first World Series Championship in 88 years, my entire family has been thrown into a frenzy. I am proud to be a Sox fan and to share this moment with my family. However, there is one person, who part of me believes had some involvement in our victory, that I wish I could share this moment with. My uncle, Edwin "Ted" Crawford, a former Chicago Police Officer of 25 years and loving husband, father, and uncle who passed away in 2002 from cancer.

I never was able to share many White Sox related moments with him, since I was still young at the time (12 years), and I only began to come into my White Sox ultra fandom in early 2004. However, I have recently been told great stories of my father and my uncle visiting Old Comiskey many times throughout the '70s, '80s, and early '90s.

I can even recall once being told a story that I will never forget:

My aunt, Catherine Crawford, who would eventually marry my uncle's brother, Quinn Crawford, was excited to be going to Disco Demolition night with my uncle. Of course, any Sox fan is familiar with what happened that night. Well, as the chaos ensued, my uncle was furious with the security doing absolutely nothing, being a Chicago cop and all. However, as he stood fuming, he demanded that my aunt stay close, and of course, her being young, she wanted to go and riot with her friends. Needless to say, it's a memory that has stuck with us for all of our lives.

I remember during his funeral one of the speakers saying that Uncle Ted was most likely in Heaven, sitting in Old Comiskey Park and complaining about the horrible play of this year's team, surrounded by the baseball greats long past. He shared a passion for the Sox that I am just starting to realize I also have.

And, as I stood on Wacker Drive today, watching the parade and celebration of this year's championship team, I could only wish that I could share this moment with him. Hopefully, I actually AM sharing this moment with him, and he is looking down on me and all the Sox fans, smiling and celebrating the first World Championship 99.9% of us can remember.

Uncle Ted, I dedicate this championship to YOU!

—Josh McReady

Dedicated to . . . my grandmother, LaDonna Slattery, who passed away on September 28, 2005. She was a lifelong Cubs fan, but more importantly, she was a lifelong baseball fan.

In an effort to remove her belongings from her home after she had passed, I came across a pack of baseball cards that I had given her as a child in a lock box under her bed. It brought me to tears knowing that she had held them all these years. This post-season was fantastic, but without her to banter with, it wasn't nearly complete.

Thank you, Grandma, for teaching me to be a fan and how to stand by my team through thick and thin. I love you and I miss you.

—35th&Florida

Dedicated to . . .

Richard J. and Eleanor "Sis" Daley.
Andy the Clown.
Willie Thompson.
Sheri Berto.
Harold Washington.
Gene Bossard.
Jack Gould.
Captain Stubby.

—howzer12

Dedicated to . . . both of my parents, Jim and Diane, for understanding how much this means to me. Rather than talk periodically, I spoke with both of them countless times over the past three weeks. They bought the newspapers, hats, shirts, and prayed every time the Sox needed a lift. My enhanced relationship with both of them epitomizes what the Sox can and have done. They (the Sox) can bring a son back to his roots and realize what it really means to have loving, supporting parents. I will never forget the phone calls and text messages I received before and after each game this fall. Having the Sox win a world championship and knowing I had two loving parents share it with me begs one question: What more can I ask for?

—kjhanson

Dedicated to . . . my dad, who many years ago convinced me that the North Side team was always a collection of stumble-bums and misfits who'd still be in the minor leagues for any other team, steering my attention and passion toward the South Side team instead. My dad's still with us, but it's a little harder to get him out to a game these days. I know he enjoyed this year as much as anyone.

—StillMissOzzie

Dedicated to . . . my dad. The promised land tastes so sweet. We did it!

—Yorke97

Dedicated to . . .my loving wife, Ruth, who is spending the holidays in the service of her country in Iraq. This championship means the world to her, just as she means the world to me.

—Deuce

Dedicated to . . .my grandfather who passed away 21 years ago on the day the World Series tickets went on sale. He was at Game 1 in 1959 and got his ticket from his brother.

I'd like to also dedicate this to my brother Tony who gave me the ticket he was fortunate to get for Game 1 of the 2005 World Series. Thanks, brother!

And I'd like to believe my grandfather played a part in my getting a ticket to Game 1 of our 2005 World Series!

GO WHITE SOX!

—The Dude

Dedicated to . . .my mom, Alice. She passed away in 2000, ironically from ALS (Lou Gehrig's Disease). She was a devoted baseball fan and, best of all, a devoted baseball mom. She adopted many of the Sox minor league players who came through Winston-Salem, including Carlos Lee, who was so kind and caring to her. Mom loved the White Sox and I know in Baseball Heaven she has enjoyed watching them win it all this year.

This one's for you, MOM!!

—NC_sox_fan

Dedicated to . . . all the White Sox fans out there today who stuck with the team through thick and thin, through all the highs and lows, and through all the disappointments. You stuck with the "Second Team in the Second City" no matter what happened on the North Side, no matter what the media said, and no matter how much grief you have taken.

Because of you, Sox fans of today, the Sox will have a loyal, dedicated, and strong base of true fans that will support the White Sox for the next 100 years.

Also, I'd like to dedicate the victory to the staff of White Sox Interactive, who provide a wonderful place for out-of-town Sox fans to stay current on the White Sox and give us a place to drown our sorrows and celebrate the triumphs.

I look forward to the opportunity to pass this moment and White Sox passion down to my kids and their kids.

—dividedsk717

Dedicated to . . . my father and mother, as well as the Big Hurt.

For my dad, because when I was born into a mixed marriage (Dad: Sox fan; Mom: Cubs fan) 16 years ago, my mom would dress me in blue and red before I knew what was happening. My dad made sure I became a Sox fan once I started to realize what was happening when I was three years old back in '93.

For my mom. She was born on September 22, 1959 (all of you here know what happened that day), and had been a Cubs fan her whole life. This season, the magic of a great regular season capped off with a World Championship finally made her one of us.

And for #35. For being my hero since that '93 season. I remember back then when everyone wanted to wear Air Jordans, but I wanted Frank's Reebok's with the Zebra Stripes. Over his 450+ home runs, I have seen about 30-40 of them in person. Frank, thanks for the memories; we're all so sorry you could not have played a larger part in this World title.

—I want Mags back

Dedicated to . . .my family (all SOX fans) back in Chicago and Mom (you would have loved this season, just like the Bulls in the '90s). Also, to my wife of 25, Barbie, for putting up with me and my passion for the greatest baseball team around—the Chicago White Sox.

I also dedicate this season to Jorie and Jack, my kids. As I watched them rooting for the SOX, it dawned on me that maybe I have done a pretty good job of parenting. Thanks to both of you!

—grizzbr

Dedicated to . . .my father; thank God he brought me up a Sox fan.

—Theanticub

Dedicated to . . .my uncle Ger, who taught me the ways of the Sox fan. He brought me to the first baseball game I can remember, a Sox game at Old Comiskey. He is probably the biggest reason that I am a Sox fan.

To Ozzie Guillen, who not only made me love the Sox and inspired me to play shortstop, but taught me to go out of your way to help and be nice to people. At spring training in Sarasota, back in the early '90s, he was the only one to stop and sign a baseball for me when my brother and I were standing in the pouring rain. A class act, great guy, and a managing genius.

—VivaOzzie

Dedicated to . . .

And now that the White Sox are World Champions, there are a few more people I'd like to dedicate this championship to ...

First, all praise, glory, and honor go to my Lord and Savior, Jesus Christ. The Lord has blessed me, us fans, and this city with a World Series championship. Even if you're not religious, or if your faith is different than mine, say a prayer of thanks to God (or whatever "higher power" you believe in) for allowing Chicago to experience such a thrilling moment as this win. It really puts this win into proper perspective when you consider that across the country, there are people who've lost their homes due to natural disasters, or lost loved ones, or something tragic in their lives that prevents them from celebrating, yet here in Chicago, we can take the time to celebrate something good for our city and for us as individuals.

Secondly, I'd like to dedicate this win to my dad. He and I didn't have a great relationship growing up, but I remember a conversation he and I had sometime in the early '80s. I remember asking him which team he liked better, and he said he leaned more towards the Sox. That helped me lean more to the Sox, too. Mind you, we lived in Broadview, which is a suburb 12 miles WEST of the Loop. It's south of Madison Street, but there wasn't a "Sox or Cubs" attitude there. I saw the Sox lose to Baltimore in '83 and cried when the Cubs blew it in '84 (I didn't know any better then, but I've more than atoned for that in 2003). It wasn't until I was older when I made the decision to be a Sox fan. In fact, it wasn't until I was covering the Cubs professionally as a sports reporter that I even stepped foot into Wrigley Field for the first time.

I'd also like to give a shout out to a guy named Pierre Chestang. He's a program director for a Christian radio station in St. Petersburg, Florida, but he was the sports director for WMBI Radio when I first started working there. He not only taught me how to request credentials for games, but he also had the faith to say, "You're going to be a star in radio someday." I'm not in radio as much as I'd like to be right now, but he believed in me. Anyway, it was through his methods that I was able to cover Sox games in the press box and meet my favorite players like Frank, Aaron, Buerhle, and a lot of people behind the scenes like Gene Honda, Katie Kirby, Christine O'Reilly, and even Jerry Reinsdorf himself. You appreciate being able to go to places only fans could dream of and would pay any price to get access to. In my position, I was able to watch batting practice, go on the field, and see the game from different angles and perspectives for FREE (other than paying $3 for a burger and fries ... but the soda in the press area is bottomless).

And finally, I'd like to dedicate this championship to WhiteSoxInteractive.com. If it weren't for this site, I'm not sure if I would be as hardcore of a Sox fan that I am now. It was because of this site and my contributions to it that helped me to be resilient against the ongoing Cubbie onslaught in 2003. It helped me to get information the mainstream press was either too naive or too lazy to research. Guys like PaleHoseGeorge, WhiteSoxWilkes, TornLabrum, and others really help me solidify my faith in this team ... and now it's paid off one-million fold. Great job, everyone ... thanks for putting out such a great forum for us White Sox fans. I'm proud of them, you're proud of them ... Chicago is proud of our World Champions.

And may they win many more World Series before the Cubs ever taste such a victory.

—hsnterprize

Dedicated to . . .my grandpa Dewayne, who was watching the Series from Heaven. He was a huge White Sox fan his whole life. I love him.

—DrGiggles

Dedicated to ...all the true Chicago White Sox fans that have been there the whole way. To those who sat in the cold and rain in the first months of the season and not leaving until the games were completely over. To those who were there when everyone doubted us. To those that wear black and white on their sleeve. To the ones that truly believed. This is for the true fans of the one and only CHICAGO WHITE SOX!!

Also to my whole family who have supported my decision to be a White Sox fan and taking me to my first games as a child despite being brought up on the North Side. And especially to my dad, who accompanies me to a couple games a year to cheer on the White Sox with me, and we will still continue throughout the years to make time to attend at least one game together and reflect on the memories we have had there. Truly this is a memorable season that none of us will ever forget.

—lizard6king6

Dedicated to ...my son, Mike, who has been a White Sox fan since his birth—almost 21 years ago. He knows how to raise my future grandchildren.

To my brother, Paul, who spent a lot of time taking his little sister to the White Sox game on Sundays—how we lived for the double headers.

To my best friend, Virg, who I met at Comiskey Park over 25 years ago.

To the many players who always took the time to sign a piece of paper, baseball, or program for all the little kids. You know how much that means to them.

To the 2005 World Champion White Sox—you guys did it. You are the representation of every Sox fan. You played with passion, with heart, with soul.

Life should not be a journey to the grave with the intention of arriving safely in an attractive and well-preserved body, but rather to skid in worn out, chocolate in one hand, champagne in the other, body thoroughly used up, totally worn out, and screaming "WOO HOO! What a ride!"

—Layla

Dedicated to . . . my uncle Tom, who rooted for the Dodgers to make the World Series in 1959 because my grandfather was a Braves fan and he didn't want any baseball arguments in the house.

—buehrle4cy05

Dedicated to . . . the working-class people on the South Side of Chicago, Bridgeport, Brownsville, and my very own Pilsen. The Sox have brought a great sense of pride to the South Side!!!

Also to my dad, who died when I was seven years old; the Sox and baseball made life a lot easier growing up! Now that I have a son of my own it is one of the greatest feelings in the world to know he witnessed all this with me. The Sox were the only thing that I loved until I had a family of my own. It's the only thing I knew!! GO SOX!!

—**pinwheels3530**

Dedicated to ...my great grandmother Nana.

Ninety-four years young and full of spunk, she thrived on harassing me after every Cubs win and/or Sox loss. I can still hear her voice and picture her face light up when I would get home from school: "Jason! Guess who won!" I would follow that up by saying something along the lines of "Cubs suck," and she would come back with "No, they don't," and we would trade shot after shot.

The stakes were always highest during the Cubs vs. Sox series every year. We usually watched the games together, even though it was a huge risk for me because I knew if the Cubs won, the nagging would last all year. She had a way of tormenting me unlike any of my friends or other relatives ever could. I tried my hardest to return the favor.

Nana passed away on December 26, 2003. I think about her all the time. When Paul Konerko made the final out of Game 5 in Anaheim, I thought about Nana. I realized she found one last way to torment me beyond any other ... she never got to see the Sox win it all.

—**skobabe8**

Dedicated to . . . my brothers Tim and Tom who have remained loyal White Sox fans through thick and thin and never wavered. To our mother who cheered wildly when Steve Garvey hit the homerun in Game 4 of the 1984 NLCS and who called long distance with tears of joy seconds after Juan Uribe fired it to Paulie in Game 4. Mom, Tim, Tom, and I thank you for making us Sox fans.

To all of those White Sox players and managers who left this world. Today, El Senor Al Lopez passed away. Somewhere in heaven, Ivan Calderon and Francisco Barrios are celebrating this World Series championship.

—MadetoOrta

Dedicated to . . . **my dad,** Allen Dickson; he passed away a few years back as described by my son, tadscout, earlier in this thread. He was a White Sox fan since the early 1930s growing up in NW Indiana in LaPorte. He was the starting catcher for his high school team destined for bigger and better teams until the fateful day he was hit by a batter, swinging a baseball bat wildly, in the knee cap driving it down into his shin. His career was ended, but his love for baseball grew.

He listened to every White Sox game, talk show, etc. on the radio, then watched them on TV when he could. He read everything he could get his hands on about the Sox and even charted the players and planned the trades the White Sox needed to make. He always knew what would happen or should have happened next.

He taught me baseball as soon as I could walk, coached my Little League and Pony League games and supported me wherever I played! He took me to several games at the old ball park in the '60s. He is the reason that my son and I are White Sox fans today!

I am sure that he watched the whole thing from heaven with Shoeless Joe, Luke Appling, and the rest of the great White Sox who have gone on, debating the plays, the players, the calls, and the celebrations of this years WORLD SERIES VICTORY!

—dadscout

Dedicated to . . . my mom, who passed away while I was 14, wherever she is—she will be celebrating for the 2005 White Sox just as much as I am. Also, I dedicate this season to my dad, who made me a White Sox fan and showed me everything I know today about the Chi-Sox. Thanks, parents.

—Ronnie Joniak

Dedicated to . . . Frank Thomas. He's the greatest player to ever don the White Sox uniform, and he's still the face of the franchise to many of us. He's the reason many of the younger generations, as myself, have become and continue to be Sox fans today. You can't help but love seeing Frank kiss that trophy and knowing he has finally got his ring.

—greasywheels121

Dedicated to …my dad, who took me to my first White Sox game in August 1961. As a result I now have a lifetime of memories.

Also to my daughter Leah. 2005 will go down as my favorite season not only because of the World Series title. Leah enjoyed everything about going to the game from the home run fireworks to yelling "charge" and being entertained by the scoreboard in between innings. She enjoyed the game as only a happy child could, and there is a child in every one of us who cheers for the White Sox.

—Dan H

Dedicated to …my mother! Who, when I became the first Sox fan in the history of my family when I was eight years old, has supported me throughout and had turned to our side about five years ago. Thanks, Mom, for the support!

—Clembasbal

Dedicated to …my grandpa, who passed his Sox allegiance to my dad, and in turn passed it to me. I wish I could have attended a game with both of them. But, forever in my mind, I will remember enjoying a trip to the ballpark with my dad.

—NonetheLoaiza

Dedicated to . . .my mother who, along with my dad, took me to my first Sox game when I was nine years old. I'm sure I was wide-eyed and open-mouthed the whole game.

All through her remaining years we would end every serious conversation between ourselves with a discussion on the current status of the Sox.

—Maximo

Dedicated to . . .Shoeless Joe, Buck Weaver, and my great uncle Mike, a lifelong Sox fan who passed on about 10 years ago.

—Whitesox029

Dedicated to . . .Ted Lyons, who played 211 seasons for the White Sox (1923-42, '46) and never saw the postseason.

—whtsx1959

Dedicated to . . .all White Sox fans, with us and departed. But most of all to my 11-year-old son; may your lifetime be filled with world championships.

—F1RaceFan

Dedicated to . . .my dad, who took time out of his day to create a passion and a love for baseball inside of his son. I love you, Dad.

—Petch

Dedicated to . . .

I have been attending Sox games since 1960. I never believed I would see a World Series Champion on the South Side. My grandfather took me to my first game at Old Comiskey. I was at the last game in the old park, the first game in the new park, there when we clinched in '93, and saw so many great games from my weekend season tix in right field. Never have I been so happy as when I watched Pods hit that homer in the rain in Game 2. It was a magic moment, and the crowd was as awesome as any time in Sox history. I love this team. I live for this. What a great ending to a perfect season. The Cubs are drooling and I am ecstatic! Go Go White Sox, I love you all!

—CubsDrool

Dedicated to . . . my grandfathers, my father, and my brother, all deceased, who passed along Sox fandom to me. Thank you, guys; I know you had a guiding hand in this championship season.

—Dubman

Dedicated to . . . John Rooney.

Thanks for teaching me how to love and be passionate about a great game and THE WORLD CHAMPIONS!

—kmadd

Dedicated to ...three people who have made the most impact on my life. First, my dad, who grew up near Wrigley and was a longtime Cubs fan, who took me to both Sox and Cubs games prior to me developing an allegiance to either and giving me an interest in the game. Second, my oldest brother, the die-hard Sox fan, who regaled me with wondrous stories of Jungle Jim Rivera, Nellie Fox, Minnie Minoso, Billy Pierce, etc., that made them seem larger than life and created a new White Sox fan for life in me. Lastly, my loving wife, a former St. Louis Cardinal fan, who tolerates this near-unhealthy infatuation I have with the White Sox and who herself has become a loyal rooter. To see the tears in her eyes on that faithful moment of the last World Series out has made my White Sox obsession all seem worthwhile.

—Buddy_Bradford

Dedicated to ...my late grandfather Mr. Emory R. Quinn. The long wait has ended. This championship is for you. Enjoy as I'm doing right now.

—rrclubfe

Dedicated to ...the **biggest White Sox fan in Maryland.**

I moved to Chicago when I was 18 in 1980. I never followed baseball until 1983 when the Sox had that wonderful season. I worked out of my truck and would listen to the games on the radio, and started to attend when I could. Saw Fisk hit one out and I was a lifetime fan at that point. Took my newborn son to his first game at Old Comiskey in 1988. I moved to California in 1990. I went to every game they played in Oakland and also attended games at Angel Stadium. Moved to Baltimore in 2000, where I now live and attend every time they are here. I watch their games on Comcast and also listen on XM radio. I collect everything White Sox, yearbooks, autographs, cards, pins, jackets, shirts, schedules, programs, posters, hats; I have an Old Comiskey seat with 45 autographs and counting. I took my whole family (my son and three girls and the wife) to opening day 2004 in Chicago. They beat K.C. this fall when they got in the World Series. My son is now 17, and I bought some real high-priced tickets and came to Chicago for both Games 1 and 2. Everybody knows what happened next; we had the time of our lives. Now I can die happy! Thank you, Ozzie, Jerry, all these great players on this team, and thank you, Chicago; no matter where I live, you're the greatest city on earth! See you all opening day. I dedicate this post to my mother who was raised in Chicago and is very seriously ill. I hope to see you all opening day at the Cell.

—sommerled

Dedicated to . . . my father and my brother. We have waited many years for this day, and I am glad I got to watch this past October with the both of you. What a season, just unbelievable.

—Jeff

110

Dedicated to ...so many people. My father, of course, because he was the one who made me a Sox fan, and all of my uncles, especially my uncle Geri with his "golden deck" in the backyard where we watched the entire Series no matter how cold or wet or late it got. Then there is my uncle Matt who is not only the biggest White Sox fan I know, he is the biggest fan of the game of baseball in general. I still remember my first Sox game ever, when I was eight, the tickets were a communion present from Matt. But most of all, I would like a special dedication to a Doherty family friend affectionately known to us as "Neighbor Al." He died from cancer the day the White Sox won the pennant and we knew they were going to the Series. Al would have loved to have been with us on "golden deck" to see the White Sox win the Series, but he was with us in spirit, and I know he was watching those games from up in heaven. This win is for you, Al.

—mdoherty2005

Dedicated to ...my father, who I lost 3.5 years ago to cancer. My most cherished and earliest memories are of him and the White Sox. He was a hardworking man who worked two jobs to provide for his family and wanted to give us nothing but the best. Fortunately, one of those gifts was the love of Chicago White Sox baseball. So many moments, it's hard to list them all. I remember him taking me and my brother to the shower in the bleachers at the old ball park on many hot summer afternoons and nights. We were also together for the furthest homer I have seen hit, and it's the homer that has led to my user name on this Web site. Kittle in

1990 hit one off of Boston's Rob Murphy that was estimated at 545 feet. My father grew up watching the best baseball had to offer, and he said that was the hardest hit ball he had ever seen.

On a funnier side, my father used to announce the plays me and my brother would make as kids when we were playing catch out in front of our house. A typical call might go like this: "Ground ball to Blomstrand. To his brother Robert at second. On to first ... double play and the Sox win!" And what is really funny to me is that if one of us took a bad hop and got hurt, he would say, "Herm Schneider out to look at Blomstrand. He has the spray out and is taking care of the injury." All the while he would be playing the part of Herm and acting like he was spraying the freeze spray on our injuries. And as God as my witness, the pain went away! How's that for mind over matter. He was treating us like real ball players. Tough ball players who played for the Sox so we couldn't keep crying. I guess there is no crying in baseball, except when the team your father has passed on to you as a love and passion finally wins it all. I know my father saw his beloved White Sox win the World Series from where he is. I know he is happy and smiling just like the family he left behind. God Bless the White Sox and all Sox fans everywhere.

—kittle545feet

Dedicated to . . .my South Side Cubs Fan Parents who took me to my first baseball game at New Comiskey in '91 to see the White Sox play because tickets were more available and Wrigley was too far from our house. As the old saying goes, two wrongs made a right, and a Sox fan was born. Fourteen years later I've never been so grateful.

—DASOXFAN

Dedicated to . . .my father, who's brooding wait (unlike mine) was measured in decades, not years.

To Chicago, a city that has accepted Super Bowl championships and two three-peats of NBA championships as conciliation prizes over the past eighty-eight years.

To Bill Veeck, for all the right reasons.

And finally, to the 2005 Chicago White Sox, who won not with large sums of money, strange chemical enhancements, or over-hyped stars, but merely by playing the game better, as a team, on the field.

—Christopher J. Falvey

Dedicated to . . .my pops for taking me to White Sox games as a kid and to the Mrs. for growing up South Side.

—donkeylips

Dedicated to . . .all of the fans. To those who have been Sox fans all their lives and had the love of this team passed down from their families to them. And, to those who are like me, North Siders with South Side hearts who grew up surrounded by Cubs fans, but saw the true light of baseball and became dedicated Sox fans at a young age. To my friends, Tim, Dan, Mark, Pat, and Jeff, who were all fans along with me, watched games with me, and celebrated with me when they finally won.

—balaspa

Dedicated to . . .both my grandfathers and my father. None was here to see this great season. They all would've appreciated this team.

—jdm2662

Dedicated to . . .my dad and my grandfather, without whom I would have never become a Sox fan. I remember going to games with both of them in the early '90s, and it was awesome. It is too bad, though, that my grandpa didn't get to see it. All his life he didn't get to see it, but I'm sure he was watching with joy from heaven. It's also too bad that my father was turned off a lot to baseball after the strike of 1994. He would have had an even bigger blast than he had with the postseason this year. So this is for Tony and Walter Pereklita. Thank you, White Sox, for a great year.

—Klita

Dedicated to . . .my dad, Gregory Gbur, a lifelong Sox fan for 53 years before his death this January of colon cancer. Whenever someone said that there was "magic" in what the

Sox were doing this year, I knew it was Dad who had something to do with this "magical" season.

—Jason

Dedicated to . . .my dad, who passed away in 1961 but planted the love of the White Sox by taking me to games starting in 1960 and watching many Jack Brickhouse calls on TV with me. My dad's favorite player was Minnie Minoso. And to my grandma and grandpa who took me to Comiskey after my dad died. Grandpa was a bus driver for the CTA and told me how to take the bus to the ballpark from our neighborhood when I was old enough to go on my own. They launched me as a lifelong White Sox fan.

—nebraskasox

Dedicated to . . .Fidel Castro, who had Jose Contreras and El Duque pitching 20 hours a day since they were six months old.

—Jenks4Pres

Dedicated to . . .**heroes and friends, lost and found.**

This championship makes me think of my #1 White Sox hero, Walt "No Neck" Williams, who signed my mitt in 1969, when I was 13 and who always— ALWAYS—hustled, no matter where he was on the playing field. His effort and dedication to excellence also epitomizes the 2005 White Sox, and I hope he's around, healthy, and can take some pleasure in this victory.

I also pay tribute to fellow members of Evanston Township High School's "White Sox Fan Club," circa 1972-73. I know my closest buddies in the club—particularly Clarence, Phil, and Benny—are as thrilled by this milestone as I am.

Finally, I acknowledge my great dad, who has never necessarily loved the White Sox (he grew up in Detroit) but has always loved the joy I've taken in the team. We went to games in the 1960s, 1970s, 1980s, 1990s, and even through to the present day. On the occasion of his 75th birthday (July 24), I flew into Chicago from D.C., and we watched the Sox beat up on Boston together. He instilled in me the joy of seeing baseball with my dad; I am so delighted I can now instill that same love in my own sons.

Life is sweet. THANKS, WHITE SOX!!

—joshua1024

*Dedicated to . . .*the Sox Nation.

I dedicate this to any and every true White Sox fan who lives and dies with this team just like I do and to the young fans of this organization who will eventually become responsible for supporting this team. I'm thankful to God for allowing me to see this.

—MVP

Dedicated to …my dad for taking me to Comiskey every summer since I was a little girl to see my Chicago White Sox. For taking me to the bar with him to see Sox games and watching them with me at home. For teaching me about this beautiful game called baseball! My first love!

Also, to Carlton Fisk, a hardworking player and my all-time favorite. Whom I always wanted to see win a championship with the Chicago White Sox!

—bgirl1975

Dedicated to …my father, who passed away in April of 2003. Bob Kuz, aka BKUZ. If it wasn't for him taking me to so many games as a child I wouldn't be the huge SOX fan I am today! Thanks, Dad, for all the memories!

—Kuzman

Dedicated to …my grandfathers. Their love of baseball both Sox and Cubs instilled a passion for baseball in me that no other sport carries. My love of the Sox came from growing up on the southwest side ('70s-'80s) of Chicago where being a Sox fan was just a way of life. The Cubs might have well played in a different state in my mind. They weren't even an afterthought. The nuns in school would tell you stories of the '59 team and how the Sox define the South Side and what real baseball was.

If you grew up in my neighborhood you were a Sox fan, Bears fan, and Notre Dame football fan in that order.

I'm 36 now, and I thank God I was born and raised on the southwest side. My life would have missed out on something unique had I grew up somewhere else.

—Lawll

Dedicated to . . .my father, his father, and his father-in-law, who as a Sox fan and a semi-pro baseball player probably saw the Sox play in both the 1917 and 1919 World Series.

—shoota II

Dedicated to . . .my father, who is now able to see his favorite baseball team celebrate a World Series. Baseball has always kept us close even though we live far apart. From when I could walk and talk, he was teaching me about the White Sox. Dad, I love you, and I'm glad we could see our team win together!

—soxfanreggie

Dedicated to . . .my two children, Tanee and Frankie, and to my wife, Lou, as we watched the World Series together as a family and cried when the last out was made. May my children someday do (and feel) the same LOVE with their own children.

And my other dedication is to my homeboys (for those still here) from 18th and Throop who in the mid '60s and early '70s we would walk to Sox park and catch a game and then spend another hour or so waiting for the players to sign autographs for us. Truly cherished memories that were re-kindled this past week.

Thank you and Gracias to the 2005 Grinders, the Chicago White Sox!!!!

—CoolPapaFrank

Dedicated to ...George Burns (the elderly, handicapped, black man that used to sit behind home plate every game) for passing away last year, going to heaven, and talking God into finally bringing a World Series title to the best city in the world! Sorry you didn't get to see it from behind home plate, George, but I'm guessing you had a pretty good view!

—fletcher1

Dedicated to ...my grandfather, Alex Maziarz, for taking me to see Dave Rozema and the Detroit Tigers on June 10, 1983. Exiting the tunnel and entering Tiger stadium for the first time and seeing that burst of green grass against the blue sky, I was hooked on baseball forever. Even though I have lived in Chicago for only five years, the Sox are now my team. I love these guys more than the '84 Tigers and will always have them in my heart. Also, to Aamir Burki for showing me the way and saving me from being a Cubs fan, a fate worse than death.

—mjn

Dedicated to . . . my **grandma, biggest fan I know,** who could spit out stats and players like you wouldn't believe. She never got to see a championship team in her life when she passed away three years ago. Grandma, this one's for you!

—wsoxgalkelly

Dedicated to . . . a lot of people. In particular, it is dedicated to all the die-hards, the types that show up to a game on a 40 degree Wednesday night in April. The types that wear their black, white, and grey with pride no matter if their team is 15 games up or 15 games back. The types that don't care if we don't have a trendy bar right across the street from our park. The types that don't care about attendance figures. The types that don't care what "Heineybirds" like Jay Mariotti crow about in the newspapers. The types that will defy the current trends to embrace a team that embraces losing. The types that post on this very message board. The types that live and die with EVERY SINGLE PITCH OF EVERY SINGLE GAME.

But first and foremost, this championship is dedicated to my dad, because without him, I wouldn't even be making this dedication in the first place.

GO SOX!!!!

We are Chicago White Sox fans, and NO ONE can take that away from us.

—SpartanSoxFan

Dedicated to ...**the '59 Sox.** Without them, the White Sox wouldn't have gotten a piece of my soul. God only knows how many little kids are out there now getting the same calling and their lives will never be the same because they will never completely lose their youth. Thank you, World Champion 2005 Chicago White Sox.

—jdieter

Dedicated to ...my parents and my sister. Whether we attended the games or watched them on television, being Sox fans was something we shared together. It brought us together and made us a stronger family.

—WestSox

Dedicated to ...my grandfather, who was at the 1932 World Series. He said there was no doubt that Babe Ruth called his homer against the Cubs, whom he was rooting against.

It's also dedicated to my dad who made me the Sox fan that I am.

Also, to my son and daughter, who carry the Sox fan torch nobly.

Also, to my wife, with whom I celebrated '83, '93, '94 (sort of), and '00.

To Harold Baines, who toiled in anonymity too long.

Finally, to my father-in-law, who watched the series from his box seats in Heaven.

—Nighttrain Wayne

Dedicated to . . . my mother. She is the reason that I am a Sox fan. Every year as a youngster we would go to the Sox opener with my granduncle. It seemed that every opener would also be on Good Friday. What does a fasting Catholic eat on Good Friday at a ball game—popcorn and cotton candy!

We saw Frank's first hit in Milwaukee and closed the old park. As I became an adult and eventually have had my own children, I have been able to give them a love of the White Sox that I got from her.

This April as the Sox began this glorious season, something seemed wrong with Mom. Her energy was lagging, much more than one would expect from a 57-year-old. In May, she was diagnosed with late-stage ovarian cancer. She has suffered this summer, but the Sox have given her and my dad something to watch and look forward to. Dad tells me she smiled when Uribe made the throw for the final out to Paulie—I would expect nothing less!

So, Mom, you always taught me to be loyal to my South Side roots and our White Sox. We got to see them win it—together. Mom, this championship is about many things but for me it was for you!!

—clarkent

Dedicated to . . . my father, Roy Johnson, who is the only bigger White Sox fan than me that I know. This is for taking me to games when I was younger, for coaching my Little League team, and teaching me the game that I love. My father and I haven't always seen eye to eye over the years, but we've always had one thing in common: The Chicago White Sox.

—Scott Johnson

Dedicated to . . .my dad. He was the person who taught me baseball, and even though we live in Deerfield, he taught me to love the Sox. He took me to so many baseball games and was the one who built my passion for the Sox. I'm at college in Ann Arbor, and I still came in for every game of the playoffs because it means the world to me. I wish he could have seen this, but at the same time I think he really did.

—sox230

Dedicated to . . .my grandfather. He has been through a lot in his life and has always been there for my brother and me through a lot of difficult times in our lives. He is a lifelong White Sox fan and has been waiting for this his entire life. I am so happy I had a chance to witness this special moment with him.

—CHIsoxNation

Dedicated to . . .everyone who wanted it as badly as I did. I can now say "I saw my favorite team win." Hopefully I'll be saying that a lot more throughout my life.

—SoxSpeed22

Dedicated to ...my mother, who passed in 2001, and my sisters, who looked up to me enough to become passionate Sox fans of their own.

—ShoelessJoe

Dedicated to ...all of the longtime Sox fans who are seeing the first championship on the RIGHT SIDE of town in 88 years. I dedicate this to the Sox fans who never had the pleasure of seeing a winner. Most importantly, I dedicate this championship to the blue-collar, die-hard Sox fans who lived for the day that they could say, "2005 WORLD CHAMPION CHICAGO WHITE SOX."

—rbeze09

Dedicated to ...the memory of my grandfather Joseph R. Nagle of Ottawa, IL.

—saltwater farmer

Dedicated to ...my father. He is the main reason my life revolves around this team. Oddly enough we have never gone to a game together. I just know I am lucky because he is still with us and that statement still has the chance to be corrected. I would like to dedicate this win to one of my best friends' (late) father, Mr. Ted Coroneos (Teddy)! He was a true and real fan. I have seen more games with them two than anyone else. From the huge Frank Thomas mirror in his basement to the best pre-game Italian beefs. I am truly saddened he missed this, but Jason (his son and my friend) just had twin boys and they got to see their team (by default) win the Series, the first Series they bore witness to. So to all that did witness this great feat, remember those who waited their whole lives (literally) to see what we are blessed enough to be a part of.

—joeywpb

Dedicated to ...my dad, the reason I am what I am today, which is a huge Sox fan. I will never forget opening day of New Comiskey. He took me out of school, and we headed down to the park with no tickets. His only concern was to somehow get me in to see that game. He wasn't concerned about whether he got in; it was all about me. We were lucky and we both were able to get in. Even though the Sox were crushed that day, it was still a great day at the ballpark and something that I will never forget. Dad, you will never know what that meant to me. Enjoy this. Hopefully one of many more to be shared ...

—joliva23

Dedicated to ...my brother Randy, who took me to my first Sox game (that I can remember).

To my cousin Emily, my only other ally in grade school; the two of us fought tirelessly against the Cubs fans who said they were better.

And to my dad, who raised me a Sox fan, whose passion for the Sox just exceeds mine and who can barely stay awake for a whole game. Love you, Dad!

—manders_01

Dedicated to ...all my fellow die-hard Sox fans who have waited so long and put up with everything that comes with cheering for the White Sox in Chicago. This includes all of those who aren't with us anymore but thrived throughout life with the help of baseball and the hope of witnessing a winner while going through all the good and bad times. This year's team is a lesson that you should never stop believing. All White Sox fans, in person or spirit, will hold a special place in their heart for the 2005 White Sox.

—Mike

Dedicated to ...my grandpa. He's been a Sox fan for as long as he can remember. He was born in 1915, so I'm pretty sure he doesn't remember the 1917 championship. I'm glad to he was able to see one before he grabs the eternal bench. I hope he sees one again next year.

—Chips

Dedicated to ...my grandfather who was born in 1919 but sadly passed away in 1988. He was a die, die-hard fan who lived White Sox baseball to the day he died. He was the first person I thought of when the final out was made.

—dpbyron

Dedicated to . . .my dad, Sox fan since the early '70s, passed that love on to me, and I don't think he realizes the positive impact. Also I want to give my Lord Jesus Christ all the glory; you may not think he cares about stuff like this but he does, about the souls and lives of the players and fans, and boy did he put some joy in my step on this one. Oh yeah, my boys Devon and Brandon, ages 9 and 11, are of course Sox fans. YES! This is to them also.

—jerry myers

Dedicated to . . .**both my grandpas.** To my one grandpa who is a die-hard Sox fan and was at Game 1 of the 1959 World Series and was able to come to Game 1 of this Series with me. And to my other grandpa who, even though he was an Indians fan, passed away this summer and was one of the main reasons I started watching baseball. RIP.

Hinrich

Dedicated to . . .all my boys from the neighborhood. We have all lived and died with this team year after year, wanting nothing more than a World Series. The Barry Bonds game from 2003 sticks out the most. After blowing the game in the ninth on a bomb by Bonds and a slam by Rich Aurilia, I took one look at the picture in the Bullpen Bar of the '93 Division clinching game with Karkovice and McKaskill and shouted:

"ALL I WANT IS A WORLD SERIES! CAN WE JUST GET ONE WORLD SERIES IN MY LIFETIME! IS THAT TOO MUCH TO ASK?"

At that time, it seemed it was light years away.

Today, that day feels like it happened light years ago...

Here's to the South Siders and the White Sox, 2005 WORLD SERIES CHAMPIONS!

—Pasqua's Posers

Dedicated to ...my grandfather who lived in the 1200 block of Belmont but was a Sox fan. One Sunday he had the White Sox game on his TV, and I sat in his lap and watched my first baseball game.

I became a White Sox fan that day and still remember my uncle calling the team Stankie's stinkies.

To my dad, who grew up on Fletcher down the street from Wrigley and NEVER paid to see a Cubs game as a kid. He would pick up papers after Cubs games to get a free ticket, or sell newspapers in front of Wrigley and then sneak in after the game started, even get in line behind Boy Scouts and march right in with them.

Once he got into high school he would go down to Comiskey Park for night games with his buddies and see the Sox battle it out with the Yankees and Indians.

My dad took me to Knights of Columbus father-and-son dinners, which always had a local sports star who you could meet up close. He always had time to play toss with me and told me to take 100 practice swings with the bat every day. I would sit and listen to my dad tell me stories about Bob Feller, Ted Williams, Joe DiMaggio, and Luke Appling. Dad came to all my games in Peanut and Little league, and took me to at least one Sox game a year.

To see the look on his face as we walked out of the Cell after Game 2 of the ALCS was special. It was like he was that little kid again who 66 years earlier did whatever it took to get into the ball park to see his heroes.

—hose

Dedicated to . . . my grandpa, who had enough sense to become a Sox fan when he moved to Chicago in the 1950s! Pap, this one's for you.

—Jeff

Dedicated to . . . all Sox fans past, present, and future. But mostly to the fans who would have loved to see a World Series title but didn't make it and who are no longer with us.

Thank you to the 2005 White Sox; you made us all very proud.

—Rikirk

Dedicated to ...the Unanders, who took me to my very first White Sox game. And Matt Unander, who's been there with me every year since.

—munchman33

Dedicated to ...my mother and father and brother who passed away. I know they were watching.

I would like to also dedicate this win to all the folks that live in the small towns of Illinois that root for the White Sox.

—krull40

Dedicated to ...

Words can't describe how this World Series has made me feel. Not only has this team accomplished something I've waited my whole life for, but they've done it with such a fantastic group of guys.

I don't think any team can embody the concept of team more than the 2005 Chicago White Sox. In the post-steroid, prima donna sports culture, this team played without ego and they won the right way. They played baseball the way it was supposed to be played, and they said to hell with the national media and anyone else that didn't believe in them.

Years of being the second team in the second city vanished. Years of watching guys like Scott Ruffcorn, Rod Bolton, Carlos Castillo, and Kirk McCaskill, forgotten!! There is no better feeling than seeing years of investment in a team gratified by bringing that trophy home.

After the game, I was walking down Michigan Avenue with my friend Munchie (Munchman33) when the police motorcade and the buses came speeding down. I ran into the street to see AJ lifting the trophy over the side of the double-decker bus and Ozzie pointing at us as if to say, we all accomplished this.

Bring on 2006.

—dogatlarge

Dedicated to . . .my father, who spent his hard-earned money for so many years on season tickets only to give them up when I went away to college. Thanks for making me a Sox fan.

—cbrownson13

Dedicated to . . .the Hawk.

—Hawk Harrelson

Dedicated to . . .my mom, for not only humoring but even participating in our family of boys' (even our two cats are guys) obsession with the White Sox.

My dad, for attending IIT so to solidify our family allegiance to the South Side (despite living in the north).

My brother, for always being able to talk baseball with me no matter what.

My grandma, for immigrating from Italy and choosing wisely when selecting a baseball team.

My other grandma, for calling me to profess her Polish pride after the AJ antics.

Every person who came up to me and wished me congratulations.

To the City of Chicago, so while I am temporarily away from home, I can show off pictures of the most scenic tickertape parade, and know that my city is "a tall bold slugger, set vivid against the little, soft cities."

—chicagoarchitect

Dedicated to . . . my parents, who made me the White Sox fan that I am today, especially for my father, who grew up amidst a family of Cubs fans.

Unfortunately my father wasn't around to watch this historic season; he passed away almost three years ago. But knowing him, one of his favorite players would have been AJ and after watching what happened during the playoffs, my dad might have been closer to the action than I thought!

For true, die-hard White Sox fans who've endured throughout the years, while staying faithful and true to the South Siders.

Last but certainly not least, for my two daughters, Jessikah and Taylor, ages four and three respectively; words can't describe how fun it was to experience this with them!

—MarkyBear

Dedicated to ...my best friend Nathan who got me interested in the Sox exclusively when I was a "Chicago fan" as a young child and the Big Hurt, Ozzie Guillen, Robin Ventura, and all the guys from the early '90s teams.

—RealMenWearBlack

Dedicated to ...my grandma, who took me to see Carlton Fisk, the greatest baseball player a six-year-old could ever see, and Harold Baines, who will always be Grandma's "boyfriend." Watching the White Sox win Game 1 of the 2005 World Series with Grandma was one of the most special things in my life, especially when I think of all the other parents and grandparents who weren't here to see the greatest season of White Sox baseball. Ever.

—Mike Harrison

Dedicated to ...my father, Michael L. Chamberlain, who took my brothers and me to hundreds of Sox games and obviously raised his seven kids to root for the right Chicago ball club. Dad passed away in April 1996. Additionally, to my brother Matt who was killed in June 1984. The last night he and I ever spent together was on Rush Street, and he and I were both sporting our new White Sox jackets as we made our rounds. I know the two of them are celebrating with the thousands of other Sox fans in heaven who've waited for this moment!

—signal00

Dedicated to . . .my dad. He made it possible for me to go to so many games, and the games we attended together are now special memories. I am glad we could become closer over baseball. I love you, Dad.

—mweflen

Dedicated to . . .my grandpa Joe who emigrated his whole family, including my mother, from Ireland to the South Side in the 1960s. Never without a Sox hat, he unfortunately was never able to see them achieve the success that he always dreamed of. Our thoughts were with you this entire run, Gramps, and we all like to think you helped give the whole team the little extra boost they needed to accomplish what they did. Thank you.

—CaptainBallz

Dedicated to . . .my grandfather Leo McIntosh. He was a raving White Sox fan until 1919 when they broke his heart. He then became a Cubs fan. Perhaps now he can be at peace.

—starboy0

Dedicated to ...my dad, Bill, who from the moment of my birth, raised me as, and taught me the ways of, a Sox fan. We've watched a lot of Sox games together and talked endlessly about the ones we watched separately. In a family full of "Cubs fans" and pseudo baseball fans, we always knew the truth and kept the faith. Glad we both got to see a White Sox championship!!

To my late grandfather from my mom's side, James, who, along with my dad, took a seven-year-old boy to his very first Sox game—the season finale of 1977. A memory that will be with me forever. I remember listening to and watching the White Sox with you on those Sunday afternoons in the summer. Another true Sox fan in the midst of Cubs fans. You've been gone 20 years now. My only wish is that you could have seen this, but somehow, somewhere, I think you did.

—SOXPHILE

Dedicated to ...my favorite and the best White Sox player of all time, the Big Hurt. Wear that ring proud, big man; you earned it!

To my dad for raising me as a White Sox fan and for taking me to countless games, including Games 1 and 2 of the World Series. I know those games will be memories I will carry with me forever. I can't describe how much I appreciate being able to share this season with you.

To my little brother who was able to see the Sox clinch in Houston. I am glad you are always there to talk

White Sox baseball with me. I am also thankful that you only had to wait twelve years for this to happen.

To the entire 2005 White Sox team, you guys are unbelievable and you have brought me so much joy this year! It was the most amazing season by any team in Chicago. Let's do it again next year!

—Evman5

Dedicated to . . .my grandfather who was a Cubbie fan, but I loved him anyway. I remember sitting on the couch on Saturday nights watching the Sox play on WGN and us going back and forth seeing who can get the best shot on each other's team. He was more than a Cubs fan to me, because he taught me the game that I have learned to love soooooo much. I can remember when we would go out to the back yard and we would play baseball, no matter if he was not feeling good that day. I like to think that even though he was a North Sider he helped my Sox pride grow like nothing has. This one also goes out to every other Sox fan that has passed away before this has happened whether I know them or not. Guys and gals, living or dead, we did it!!

—crazyozzie02

Dedicated to . . .my dad, Brendan O'Leary. He came over from Ireland in the '40s and was a long and suffering Sox fan.

He battled his cancer viciously this month and succumbed, but he held on to see the Sox win it. It was the last thing I got to tell him. Eight hours after they won it, he passed. I am convinced if it went 5, 6, or 7, he would have held on to see them win.

His last words to me: "They are a great team; they will do it."

Thank God he got to see it.

—**caracascat**

Dedicated to . . . **my dad and brother.**

Originally I thought my grandfather had not seen the Sox win a World Series but I forgot he would have 17 in 1917. So he knew the joy I felt when the Sox won it all.

My grandfather would come over to our house and watch games while drinking a shot of whiskey and a bottle of Diet Rite and eating Mr. Salty pretzels.

He passed away in 1977.

My dad was there in '59. He loved Ozzie because he played hard. My dad was a popular shortstop in his day playing softball (16 inch).

He passed away in 1987.

I never knew my brother because he died when I was three. But I know he loved baseball as I have seen family photos of him with his cap on.

He passed away in 1968.

I love the way this game strings together the many generations of fans.

—**MarkPloch**

Dedicated to . . . BOB ELSON, the original "commander." He worked as the Sox radio announcer for decades and spent 40 years covering and announcing in Chicago. He made the games come alive (even those that were called off the Western Union tickertape) without being a homer or fan whore. He was inducted into the Hall of Fame, but didn't live nearly long enough to see this day. God Bless you, Bob.

—**AZSoxFAN**

Dedicated to . . . my grandfather who came over from Italy. He couldn't read or write either Italian or English. He was an avid, die-hard White Sox fan and listened to every game on the radio. My grandfather lived around 36th and Damen, maybe a 10-minute bus ride from Comiskey Park. My parents bought him a color TV in the late '60s and it didn't matter. He kept listening to every game on his transistor radio. Once, my grandfather took me to a game against the Angels. It was Shriner day. We were the only two not wearing a Fez in the crowd. The Sox lost 6-1, but it was a great day anyway. He died in 1972. If he were alive today, my grandfather, who was very stoic in the old country way, would not have said much to us about this year. I just know he would have been smiling and proud inside. After the Series ended, my father said, "This one is for you, Pops. I wish he was here to see this."

—jimlandis55

Dedicated to . . .

There was a very old South Side guy who was in a TV beer commercial during the either the 1969 or 1970 season, two of the worst in Sox history. I was only about five, but I remember that the Sox were on WFLD-TV, and in the commercial (I think for Meister Brau) then-announcer Jack Drees asked the guy what he thought of the White Sox. The old guy (who IIRC had on a Sox cap and jacket and thick glasses and must have been at least 80) said something like if the Sox picked up a home run hitter and a couple of pitchers, they could win the pennant and maybe even the World Series. Which he pronounced "World Serious."

I'd dedicate the 2005 Championship to him and to everyone like him—there must be millions of them—who came and went and were good Sox fans the whole time, even though it was never easy, and who never saw the Sox win another pennant let alone a World Serious.

I'd also dedicate it to the Mrs., who sat through 5+ hours of absolutely miserable weather even though she (a) doesn't like baseball and (b) was three months pregnant, to watch the second game of the World Series. I told her it was probably the greatest day in White Sox franchise history. Which it was, until Wednesday, October 19, 2005, rolled around.

And to Bobby Smith, who introduced me to baseball in 1967 (when I was four) when he gave me a spare Tommy McCraw baseball card. There was no turning back after that.

—jackbrohamer

Dedicated to . . .my mother, Louise, who passed away in '98, after dealing with my father and me.

I believe she guided Blum's Home run in the 14th.

It would have been her 80th birthday that day.

—soxwon

Dedicated to . . .my grandfather Harry Tannehill, who passed away in March and was buried with a White Sox cap; and to my father, Brian, who took me to my first Sox game and about 20 games this magical season including the World Series.

—Chris Tannehill

Dedicated to . . .my big brother Jose, who was a father figure and a mentor in my adolescence. The one who made me buy packs of $.50 bubblegum baseball card sets and read every stat from a White Sox player. The one who showed me the ropes of Comiskey Park and the history of this great organization.

This championship is dedicated to the working man that my brother dictates. He is the common knowledgeable old-school kind of fan you will find. One of many thousands who wanted to attend the World Series but could not afford the high broker prices.

At a distance we didn't get to watch the Series together, but at heart we shared the same passion for the good guys. Big bro, you dreamed of this for a long time and now it finally came true; this WSC is dedicated to you.

—**Shorty1983**

Dedicated to . . .my husband, Mick, who passed away from cancer last May. I feel in my heart that he is one of many angels in heaven that were rooting our White Sox on! Miracles do happen!

—**Soxmissy**

Dedicated to . . .a bunch of different people:

To every fan who was there for all of the home opener in 2003, watching Esteban Loaiza pitch after a 2-hour rain delay in 40-degree rain and sleet. And every fan who has sat through a weeknight game in awful weather, bundled up and refusing to leave no matter what the score.

To every young kid in Chicago who will be growing up in a different baseball world than we have lived in all our lives. May you be the next generation of proud Sox fans flying the flag high.

To the fans who were out in the bleachers with my family members in the '70s, which from what I'm told is a small amount a lot of the time, thanks for keeping the passion there when everything looked dark.

To all the players who will never have their numbers on the wall or be in Cooperstown. To the Greg Hibbards, the Scott Fletchers, the Joe Cowleys, the Floyd Bannisters, the Lance Johnsons, thank you for being the people I rooted for growing up.

To my grandfather James J. Nolan (1928-2004), who watched so many games with me. Who gave me the love of *watching* baseball, of really watching every pitch for how it fits into the tapestry of the game as a whole. I wish you could have been here; you would have loved this team even more than 1990 or 1977 or 1959. When I brought a small bag of his ashes to the park and spread it along the third base foul area, I looked to the sky and said, "Well, one of us has to keep watching this team so we can celebrate a World Series one of these years." This year, I celebrated for the both of us. Thanks, Gramps. This one is for you.

—**spiffie**

Dedicated to ...my wife, who passed a few years back. We met at a White Sox game and held season tickets together for almost ten years.

I still carry the same tickets and sometimes leave her seat open as I feel her presence at the games sometimes.

My health is fading fast these days, and when I pass, we will watch the goings on together once again.

—harwar

Dedicated to ...three people who are no longer with us. My grandfather John, who passed on many years ago, was a big Sox fan who started off the family in the right direction ... cheering on the Sox. My grandmother Sophia, who also loved the Sox and would watch many games with the family. And last but not least, my uncle and godfather Wally (the beerman) Wrona. You couldn't be more of a die-hard Sox fan than he, but he sadly passed on two years ago. He would have loved to see this day, but it just never came to pass. On the day the Sox won the World Series I wore his Sox jacket to Bourbon Street and then out to Bridgeport. So even if he wasn't down here for the win in person, he was in spirit. God bless them, and God bless the Sox.

—WSox8404

Dedicated to ...

I don't even know what to say. For my entire life I've lived being the fan of "the teams that never win." My favorite NHL team, the St. Louis Blues, have never won a Stanley Cup Championship in their history, and the Chicago White Sox hadn't won a World Series since 1917 (only a mere 88 years ago). But now, I'm proud to say that I'm a fan of the 2005 World Series Champion Chicago White Sox. I've followed these guys as long as I can remember, stuck with them through thick and thin, waiting for this particular moment. Right from spring training this past season I felt there was something special about this particular group of guys; their desire to win and their attitudes toward one another. They were like a big family; everyone got along and enjoyed being together. This team is made up of a bunch of relatively "no-name" guys, save for a few. There are no real superstar egos on this team; it's just a bunch of tough, hard-playing guys who went out day after day playing their hearts out to get the W. Well, they battled all season and got it done the right way.

This one is for the Chicago White Sox organization— the staff, the fans, everyone. This one is for the players. They are the ones who made this happen. You guys are all awesome and deserved this more than anyone. You made many dreams come true.

Congrats, again, to all the fans who've waited and stuck with the team throughout the years. I know many have waited a lot longer than I have, and this one is for them.

This is truly amazing.

When I woke up the morning after the World Series ended, the first thing I did was look for the newspaper, more importantly, the sports page to make sure of one thing:

... It wasn't a dream.

2005 WORLD CHAMPIONS!!!!!!!!!!!!

—ViPeRx007

Dedicated to . . .

In 1960 I went to my first Sox game against the Orioles. Jim Landis hit a home run and the Sox lost 2 to 1. The thing I remember most though was walking in that night and looking at that field and that scoreboard. It truly was a beautiful sight. Throughout the next decades, the Sox were my life. Living and dying with each game until the end of September. I'll have a silly grin on my face this entire winter until spring training starts again. What a feeling. I thank my mom for getting to me first (Dad was a Cubs fan) so I dedicate this to her, but also to every Sox fan who wasn't around to experience this. Unbelievable!

—jvoboogie

Dedicated to . . .

So many thoughts passed through my mind that night the Sox won the World Series. As I stood there cheering that last out, all I could think about was my previous 46 years of being a White Sox fan. You see, it was my dad that took me out of school on opening day in 1960 so I could attend my first game. All I ever knew about baseball before that was that I was still pretty bad at it as an eight-year-old. I will never forget the feeling that came over me as I walked up the steps from under the stands at Old Comiskey Park. The colors were so bright and beautiful. It was to be the first of many games my dad and I would go to during the '60s. I fell in love with the Sox right away as they won that game against Kansas City. To my dad, who passed in 1999, I will always be grateful for the time we spent together at Comiskey.

I also think of my mom. Born in 1917, she obviously never saw a championship team, but was a huge Sox fan too. She would have loved how the team of 2005 played.

I have raised two sons, now both in their twenties and off on their own. We have spent countless nights and afternoons together at both ballparks. I took them there to introduce them to the Sox while they were still in diapers. Even though one of them has relocated to St. Louis, he remains to this day an avid Sox fan and loves the game so much he continues to toil in the minor leagues, hoping to reach the majors some day as a pitcher. My sons and I have that special bond between a father and a son, that common bond known as White Sox baseball. We talked almost daily by phone to discuss the playoffs.

To my best friend, Ron. Thanks for being there for 46 long-suffering seasons, through thick and thin, through every missed opportunity and error. This championship is also for you!

Who can forget those men that went the extra mile to ensure that the Sox would still be located in Chicago in 2005. I have lived though at least three different potential franchise shifts, where the Sox almost moved out of town. Thanks to Governor Thompson, Bill Veeck, John Allyn, Jack Brickhouse, and countless others that fought to keep the team in Chicago.

Lastly, I want to thank my wife of the past four years, Debbie. Born and raised a Cubs fan on the North

Side, she started going to Sox games with me in 2000. We are season ticket holders, and over the past few years she has finally seen the light and converted to the White Sox. She can't stop talking about their championship run and cried like a baby the night they won the world championship. I am indeed blessed to have shared this year with loved ones that love both me and the Sox!

Let's do it again in 2006!!

—DannyCaterFan

*Dedicated to . . .*all the White Sox players of the past who played their hearts out trying to be world champions. Also dedicated to all of us fans who have waited many years. I have waited 30 years for this.

I have been a Sox fan since 1976 while on vacation in Sarasota, Florida, during spring training. I got the autographs of half the players on the 1976 team, and that started a lifetime love affair with the Chicago White Sox. I arrived in Sarasota as a Detroit Tiger fan and left as a fan for life of the White Sox.

2005 WORLD CHAMPION CHICAGO WHITE SOX!!

—gowhitesox

*Dedicated to . . .*my dad, who took me to my first game way back in the '70s, when we wore the red pinstripes. As a kid, he told me about the Sox of the 1950s, the '59 Go Go Sox, Jungle Jim Rivera, the Exploding Scoreboard, Harry

Caray, Dick Allen, Jimmy Piersall. I was so ready to attend my first game that when I finally entered the old ballpark from the RF side, it is now etched into my memory forever. I thought a lot about my dad during those last three outs in Houston.

I think about all those Sox fans I saw and met while on road trips to see our beloved. In old Tiger Stadium, in the Metrodome, the THOUSANDS that showed up in '03 at Kauffman Stadium in KC. The tons of fans at the Jake in 2000 and 2001, all of us brazenly chanting and cheering our favorite players as they batted, all of the West Coast Sox fans that were at Dodger Stadium, all there despite the media telling us that a more important series was taking place back home. No, I was nearly teary-eyed at the thousands of Sox fans that showed up to Dodger Stadium in LA in '03, all wild, rowdy, boisterous, and all there to see our team. And of course, all those same fans that showed up in force and in much bigger numbers than I expected to Petco Park in San Diego. We were very loud, and Padre fans knew we were there. It was so much fun to hear everyone's story on how they got there, where they lived, how they became Sox fans, and just how much we really do have in common with one another. Sox fans make the effort. I even came up with a mathematical number to separate us from the others ... 10/50. Ten of us sound like 50 of them. Another team's fan came up to me and said, "You guys are pretty loud," and it was the best compliment I've ever gotten.

Mostly though, I think of all those who have passed before, and weren't able to see this in person. I even thought about George Burns, that handicapped guy from the far West Side of Chicago who also loved the Sox very much, and basically went to every game, taking a couple buses and the green line to the game, watching by himself. Going through all that "trouble" just to see the team he loved and cared about. He was what we all are: dedicated, loyal, intelligent, and loud.

—Hangar18

Dedicated to . . .my dad, the biggest reason I became a Sox fan.

He passed away July 4, 1992, a year after we shared some great memories in the new park with a 27-game ticket package.

I can't help but think it was my dad, and the other loved ones of members of this site who are no longer with us, that brought the rain with tears of joy as thousands celebrated in Lot C after the Sox won it all.

—CHISOXFAN13

Dedicated to . . .Papa, who in 1959, took my dad out of school and brought him to Comiskey for the World Series, and to Grampa Bob, a fierce White Sox fan who always taught us that the South Side was more than just a part of town. To both of you watching ... they did it.

And definitely for my dad, Ed Miller. In 1993, I went with my dad to Game 6 of the ALCS against Toronto. They lost. Looking at the playoff ticket prices this year, I honestly don't know how he ever afforded it, but I will remember that game for the rest of my life. He has lived and died with this team for his whole life, and he's raised my brother and me to be loyal and intelligent baseball fans.

After the Sox won the title, I raised my glass and toasted to my father and my two grandfathers for all they've done. When I told this to my dad the next day, I could hear him getting choked up on the phone. I knew then how much this team has connected all the generations of men in our family, and more importantly, how lucky we both felt to experience this season together. Thanks.

—MM2112

Dedicated to . . .my daughter, who in her zest to be the best Sox fan at age 15, cried right alongside her long-suffering mother in seeing the impossible dream achieved.

My father was the one who introduced me to the Sox, pre-birth, and took me to at least one game a season. Living in Iowa it makes it a little harder to access the games, but I have continued this tradition with my children, who attend with me at least one game a year.

Shelby was a Sox fan pre-birth, just like her mom, and yells at the TV right alongside of me, and admits to a small crush on Joe Crede, even if he is married.

The tears of joy were long overdue, and I am so thankful for the opportunity to see this come to fruition. Thanks so much to all of you who made it possible. You have my gratitude.

—digdagdug23

Dedicated to . . . my old buddies who were, as most of us, long-suffering fans. I want to dedicate this to my boyhood friend Jerry who cheered with me when Tommy Agee stole a base or hit a homer.

I want to dedicate this to Willie, Tom, and Bob in Michigan City. They felt the sting of all those fruitless years in the '70s with me.

But most of all, to Mom, who was born and raised on the South Side, and who supported my convictions all these years. She was born in 1920, and at 85 she finally saw these White Sox as champions! This is to you most of all, FiFi.

—jgreavel

Dedicated to . . . my friend Jim Sedgwick. He was a true mentor to me as we taught together in the Peoria Public Schools during the 1980s. Both of us were avid Sox fans, Jim holding more credentials as he had grown up on the Sox side and I was relative late comer, having fallen in love with the team during the wild ride of '77.

Jim told wonderful stories of Jungle Jim and Minnie, Billy Pierce, Nellie, and all the others from the Go Go era. Together we cheered on the '83 team—I remember Jim bringing in a portable black and white TV and the two of us sneaking glimpses of a day game during the '83 playoffs.

Jim was one of the most warm-hearted guys you'd ever want to meet. He was great with the special needs students with whom he devoted his professional life.

He passed away four years ago, very suddenly. I'm still shocked. It was such a loss.

Nobody would have enjoyed the 2005 championship more than Jim, and nobody would have been more fun to enjoy it with.

And, so, Jim Sedgwick, this World Series is for you! God bless your family and all of those who you touched in your meaningful, wonderful life.

—jehosaphat

Dedicated to ...my cousin John Beckman, who died last year way too young. I would bump into him at games he was at with his son.

To my good friend Bob, who sits next to me at each game on our ticket package.

To my son, Jake, who is only one year old right now but will someday hear all the stories about this year.

To my wife, Cheryl, who has put up with my obsession for years and completely understands what this means to me.

To all the Sox fans who have come before me and passed the torch along to us. I will carry it on to my son and to the future Sox fans the same way.

—zach23

Dedicated to ...all North Side Sox fans who now have one easy response to all Cubs fans: 1908! Also to my dad and all long-suffering Sox fans.

—Ishmookie

Dedicated to ...my **mother.**

Bill Veeck sent a four-piece band into the stands to play "Happy Birthday" to my mother, who, from that day on became one of the most rabid of White Sox fans. She died before she could see her dream of a White Sox world championship, but, you know what? My mother's tears flow as readily as mine now that OUR team has made it to the top. Happy many birthdays, Mom. You deserve this.

—Rhumdog

Dedicated to ...

What a great, great feeling. In my eyes baseball is life. It is played every day just like real working people do. It is an everyday grind. It is about family. My family was raised with baseball and the White Sox. My brothers and sisters have all grown up with baseball, and now we have brought that down to our kids as well. Everyone in my family are die-hard Sox fans, and I would like to thank my father for bringing us all together for this. I, like many fans, can only wish he was still alive to see this. It would have meant a lot. Thank you, White Sox, for this championship and bringing all of us together.

GO YOU WHITE SOX!!!!!!!!!!!

—Rich Cescato

Dedicated to . . .my grandfather for starting the Sox tradition in our family. He grew up in Cicero, IL, which means he was a South Sider the day he was born. He saw the 1917 World Series so he could die a happy man but was unfortunate enough to not see the 2005 Chi Sox. So I dedicate this World Series to my grandfather Jim Carmignani. Thanks for making my dad make me a Sox fan. Go Go White Sox!!!

—chubz5601

Dedicated to . . .all those I've hugged recently in celebration of a common goal. To my father, who remembered '59 and was deeply afraid until the last out. And to my good buddy Nick, that fool of a Cubs fan. I know you look down on me from heaven and curse the Sox. I hope your curse gets broken soon. I will finally root for your team now, if only a little. I'm just glad we got there and got there first.

—wags1978

Dedicated to . . .my good friend Kent, who passed away from cancer in July at age 22. I also have been dating his little sister for three years. He felt like family to me. He was a big Sox fan, and I wish he could've seen the amazing finish to this amazing season. He always wore this awful ugly sweater that had the 1989 "White Sox" script logo knit into it. His sister wore it throughout the playoffs. We all miss you, Kent.

And of course to my old man who made me a Sox fan. Thanks to you, I've wasted huge amounts of time, money, and energy, been put under stress, and ridiculed. All that suffering made it so much sweeter, but I'm sure you know that way better than I do. Thanks, Dad.

—ihatethecubs

Dedicated to ...my grandfather who passed away in 1999 and never got to see the Sox win a World Series. He was born the same year they last won and was lucky enough to get tickets to the '59 series.

He made my dad a Sox fan who in turn made me a Sox fan. I attended my very first game when I was seven years old in the inaugural season of New Comiskey. I have lived and died with the White Sox ever since.

I was lucky enough to attend Game 1 of the 1993 ALCS, only to see the Sox lose to Toronto.

I became a "regular" at Comiskey in 1994 and literally cried when the strike occurred. I couldn't believe it because I just had a "feeling" the Sox would win it all that year.

I watched with dismay as the Sox could never really put anything together in '95 and '96.

We purchased season tickets in '97, and I had a great summer! That is, until the now-infamous "white-flag" trade. That event left a bad taste in my mouth, and we refused to renew our tickets, even though my allegiance never wavered.

I still attended games in '98 and '99, just not nearly as many, and most of the games were painful to watch.

I thought 2000 was going to be the "year." I was lucky enough to attend Game 1 of the ALDS, only to go home upset. I watch the Sox get swept in Seattle with a stunned look of disbelief on my face.

2001 saw me start attending games with my prior regularity, and I enjoyed some of the best games of my life (the July 4th comeback against Minnesota and Carlos Lee's walk off against the Cubs), although the season again ended in disappointment.

The only real highlight of 2002 was watching the Sox come back from an 8-0 deficit to beat the Cubs, truly amazing!

2003 built great memories for me. I followed the team to Toronto in July. I followed them to Texas in April. I quit my job at the time to be at Comiskey for the late stretch run games against Minnesota and Kansas City, only to see my hopes bruised again.

2004 was one of the more painful years for me, seeing the Sox swept by the Cubs at Wrigley, and watching their division lead disappear after being swept at home by Minnesota.

I was one of the many fans who thought that the Carlos Lee/Pods trade was a HUGE mistake. I have never been happier to eat my words. In 2005, I attended my first game on May 1st against Detroit and saw the Sox win 8-0. From that game on, I attended nearly as many games as I did in '97 when I had my season tickets.

There were a few low points, but they were offset by the numerous HIGH points! I was fortunate enough to attend Games 1 and 2 of the ALDS and Games 1 and 2 of the ALCS. And although I could not get tickets for the World Series, I made sure I was in the city during EVERY game, because I needed to be around my fellow Sox fans, ones like me who would feel every emotion in their heart.

The day after the Sox won the World Series, I put in my deposit for season tickets for the 2006 season. I don't really have the money to afford this; if I did, I would be a season ticket holder every year and follow the team all over the country. I am going to find a way to pay for these though, no matter what.

There are not enough words to describe how grateful I am to this team for what they did in 2005. October 26, 2005, was the greatest day of my life. I have never been happier. Thank you, White Sox, for everything this year; you guys will never know how much you mean to some people. I dedicate this to my late grandfather and my die-hard Sox fan parents! Thanks for truly being the highlight of my life!!!

—Soxfanspcu11

Dedicated to . . .my aunt Mary Ann. I was her first nephew, and I treated her to what turned out to be the division clincher in 1993 (her first and only game in the new park; she thought Bo Jackson's home run would go foul, while I thought it would be caught by the left fielder; of course it kept carrying and carrying and carrying ...). She also attended the last night game in Old Comiskey Park with my mother and myself (as well as numerous games with us while I was growing up; it was good to

157

be from the neighborhood! I believe she was 10 years old when the Sox won the pennant in '59). Sadly she passed away nine years ago, but I know she's looking down and enjoying our World Championship for all it's worth. I'll also dedicate it to my grandmother (passed away in 1988). Miss you both!!!

—RadioheadRocks

Dedicated to . . .

I've been blessed; I still have all four grandparents and both parents all in good health. Never really had to deal with much personal tragedy, aside from a few family friends. I am fortunate enough to have most of the people I loved growing up still with me to this day.

Still, this win is for me and my dad. He immigrated to America from Germany in the 1950s when he was just a few weeks old. My grandfather and dad used to go to games all the time down at Comiskey Park and root for his favorite player growing up, Pete Ward. They'd tell me stories about the sirens in 1959, Harry Caray broadcasting games from the bleachers, etc.

My mom and brother are both die-hard Cubs fans, so the fact that my dad and I are the Sox fans in the family makes the bond special for us. I remember going to many games with my dad at Comiskey/the Cell; all the way from 1993 to this summer. We were there during the spontaneous standing ovation the team got at its first game back after their seven-game sweep in Cleveland and New York. After Herbert

Perry's homer gave Kip Wells the support needed to win his masterpiece, I knew right then and there that the 2000 White Sox were going to win the World Series and it would be something I could share with my dad forever.

It didn't work out that way. This summer and now I have been living in Peoria, going to school and working, away from my family and hometown. Through the magic of technology, though, my dad and I have been able to keep in touch, and we called each other almost immediately after every game, to talk about the Sox and chat about life. I really do feel we're as close as we've ever been. In a perfect world, we would have been together at a bar, sharing beers when Uribe made the last out of the season. Instead he called me almost immediately after the game ended as we both celebrated.

Thanks, '05 Sox, for giving me and my dad something to start a conversation with.

—doublem23

Dedicated to . . .my favorite Sox-loving fan, Jason. Three years ago, he not only introduced me to the #1 team in Chicago, but he showed me true pride, loyalty, appreciation, and passion for a team that has meant so much to him for so long. I have him to thank for all of the great memories that will last me a lifetime. I will share stories from this magical season for many years to come. Thanks for showing me the meaning of a true die-hard. This season is for you!

—converted

Dedicated to ...everyone at WSI, easily the best baseball fan board around.

Especially to the architects, PHG and FWC, for putting up with countless nights of troll busting and FOBB bashing. For gutting out the massive "Friends of Choice" debates, and dealing deftly with Dark Clouds and bandwagoners alike. Especially for running a clean ship. Your work has really paid off. This is the best site I've ever found.

I have some special dedications to specific posters here:

For Jerry_Manuel, who made me laugh my ass off continuously.

For doublem23, whose "Jesus-Royce" picture perfectly captured the debate.

For Jjav829 for being a fellow fantasy geek.

For Nellie Fox for being just a damn good guy.

For Daver for being just a damn good guy.

For King Xerxes for making me laugh ...

Gawd, there's a ton of others. I feel bad only recognizing the few of you. Congrats, guys. This one was sweet. Enjoy it.

—ma-gaga

I was extremely excited by the phenomenal performances and the sweep during the World Series. The team exceeded my expectations. However, this would not be possible without the experiences of one day. I remember the first game I attended at Old Comiskey. While I cannot recall specific details about the game or even the team the White Sox were playing, I remember the most important details. I remember driving down to the park with my grandpa and seeing the kids playing in the fire hydrants. I remember the Dove bar and hotdogs. I remember learning to remove peanuts from their shells before you eat them. Someday when my children ask me why I'm a White Sox fan, I can tell them about that game and how I'm a White Sox fan because of my grandpa.

—3rdgensoxfan

*Dedicated to . . .*my late grandmother, Lilly Wade Joseph.

They called her "Billy." She was born and raised in Weir, Mississippi, the same town Roy Oswalt is from, and was in fact friends with Roy Oswalt's grandmother. She moved to Aurora, Illinois, in her twenties and became a die-hard White Sox fan soon after. Her devotion was passed down to my father, and then to me. Grandma Joseph started the whole Sox thing in my family. She passed away in mid-August, and unfortunately missed out on the World Series victory by two months. But it was her founding passion for the Sox that ultimately allowed me to celebrate this title, along with my dad and my brother

161

... and as the celebration was going on, I was thinking of her, thinking of the reason I am a Sox fan, of the beginning.

Here's to you, Grandma. We won the whole damn thing!

Go Sox!

—FoulTerritory

Dedicated to ...my buddy Scott, my friend Jimbo, and my sister Rose.

Thanks for everything, and here is to our 2005 World Series Championship Chicago White Sox. Wire to Wire! WISSKI.

—BWISNIEW

Dedicated to ...my grandmother and grandfather, Mr. and Mrs. Wesley V. Pipher Sr., formally of Homewood-Flossmoor. They were great sports fans and loved the Sox, and my grandmother, who came to Chicago in 1919, although she lived to be 97 saw them in the Series just once more, forty years later, ten years after my grandfather had passed away. Every year was a new beginning and a chance that the Sox would make it back, and every season ended without us attaining the goal. However I know they saw us win it all. The nostalgia that came with the World Series took me back to kindergarten and so many fond memories that I can't be thankful enough. A truly wonderful feeling of sheer joy and happiness mixed with a bit of melancholy! I wouldn't trade it for anything, except to share it with them, and I did that anyway! No one can ever take it away from us. How truly sweet it is to say ... World Champion Chicago White Sox! God bless them all.

—**Cal Pipher**

Dedicated to ...Grandpa, who has been gone a while now; the "bums" finally did it!

—**Dickie Kerr**

Dedicated to ...my dad, Jay.

He's been taking me to Sox games since I was just weeks old. In fact, he's very proud of telling people about my first two baseball games. Game one was at Old Comiskey; I stayed awake for the entire game, and the White Sox won. Game two was at Wrigley; I slept through most of it, and the Cubs lost.

He knew from that point on I was going to be okay.

Since then, we've gone to more White Sox games than I could ever begin to count. One memorable game was in 1993, when our car broke down on the drive from the Quad Cities to Comiskey. To make matters worse, it was the hottest day of the year. We eventually managed to get the car to a neighborhood several miles away from the park, and ended up walking and taking buses to make it to the game. We were late, of course, and as we walked in we heard the crowd erupting as Frank Thomas hit one of his

163

trademark homers. It ended up being the only offense the Sox had that night, as they fell to the Angels in a pretty awful game.

I consider myself so incredibly fortunate and blessed to have watched some of the playoff games with him this year. I'm currently away at school but made several treks home to catch some games with him. And I think that's probably what I'll remember most about this season.

Thanks, Dad!

—hi im skot

Dedicated to . . . my grandfather, age 84, who finally saw his first World Championship.

My dad was born in India, and while baseball wasn't in his blood, it was in mine, and my grandfather taught me everything he knew. My only regret is that I wasn't in Chicago to watch the final out with him, to see the look on his face when a lifelong wish was finally fulfilled.

We'll still take it though. After 88 years, there's no point sweating the small stuff.

—samram

Dedicated to . . . my uncle and grandfather who did not live to see this.

To my Dad who raised me a die-hard Sox fan.

—throwsoftjax

Dedicated to …my father, who raised me to be a Sox fan and taught me to be loyal and faithful, and who didn't live to see this.

My friend Jacquie, who should have lived to see this and would have been as thrilled as I was.

My brother, who made sure I was at Game 2 and experienced one of the great World Series games of all time.

The city that never quits on its teams!

—westcoastfan

Dedicated to …my parents, for taking me to my first game in 1982, even though we left early because it rained, and I was promised a foul ball from the college students who were sitting behind us. Oh well, at least Luzinski hit a homer. Secondly, I'd like to dedicate this to my sisters and all my good friends and girlfriends who have put up with my Sox obsession for as long as they've known me. Here's to you, and here's to our World Champs!!!

—longshot7

Dedicated to …my brother Rigo, my high school teacher Mr. Raymond Bava, and the Kisielentes lifelong Sox fans.

—ghostfacesox

Dedicated to . . . my grandpa, who passed away November 1st. He finally got to see the Sox win.

Frank, you will be dearly missed, my friend; COME BACK next year!

—BigHurt359300

Dedicated to . . . my dad, "Frank," who brought his new wife and baby daughter from Italy to Chicago in the wake of World War II. He taught us American culture, English, and the White Sox simultaneously. He made rabid fans of us both. He would have enjoyed this season.

To my mom, Lee, who underwent a triple bypass in May of '04 and returned to the ballpark to cheer on our heroes a short three weeks later. She taught me more about the finer points of baseball than Dad did! Almost 84 now, she had some trouble getting to the ballpark for the playoffs but, always a Sox trooper, she made it through fair weather and foul.

To the Dominican sisters who taught at St. Philip Neri School on 72nd Street. They allowed TVs to be brought into our classrooms (almost unheard of in '59) so we could watch the games—under the proviso that we do our desk-work "or it gets turned off!" Needless to say, we kept working.

To Nellie Fox, hero of my childhood, whose greatness was obvious to the White Sox faithful. Regrettably, he did not live to see it finally acknowledged by the Hall of Fame in 1997.

To the members and friends of Sox Fans On Deck who have gone on to God's grandstand: Judith Helm; Guy Palermo; Les Sugarman, who shared his stories of being a Sox batboy in the '20s; Ron Hess, who fought a brave battle against cancer; and George Burns, who never saw his wheelchair as a place of confinement but rather a vehicle for taking on challenges.

Lastly, to my kids, Tony and Gina, and to my nephews, Jeremy and Jay, who were informed of their proud baseball heritage early in life. They will forever be Chicago White Sox fans.

I love you all!

—BiancaCalzini

Dedicated to . . .my dad who is the reason I am a Sox fan.

To my wife who made many weekend trips to Chicago for the last season in Comiskey.

To my sons who made the 2005 baseball season fun.

—Reichardt

Dedicated to . . .Pops, who took me to all my Sox games as a kid; thank you. You made me a Sox fan.

—windycityson

Dedicated to . . .my grandfather, who followed Nellie Fox through the minors all the way to Comiskey.

To my sons, who like their grandfather and father, have stuck with our Sox through thick and thin.

—Mark Olson

Dedicated to . . . John C. Rodgers, junior and senior, my grandfather and dad, who were both lifelong South Siders and Sox fans. They took me to many games with their friends from the early '60s, when my family had moved back to Chicago.

Though I was barely in grade school, I had immediately switched allegiances from the Milwaukee Braves (who had won when my mother was pregnant with me) when we arrived in Chicago. Dad, Grandpa, and I would stand in line at Sears each year to get tickets when they went on sale (Ticketmaster?). I started drinking beer around the same time at baseball games by stealing theirs when they weren't looking as the Go Go Sox played teams like the hated Mantle/Maris/Yogi/Whitey Ford Yankees, which were the toughest tickets to get back then.

Grandpa, a WWI vet and the last of our family to have seen a Sox championship until now, died in the late '60s. Dad just passed away a few years ago with colon cancer.

To my father-in-law, Donald Seahausen, who played for the single A Sox team as a young man until an injury gave his father the opportunity to draft him full-time into the family grocery business. Don greatly reveled in the Sox this year all season long and finally

168

in the Sox championship, which he's waited all of his eighty years for.

To Bill Veeck and family (Mike, Lisa, et al), whose dedication to the game and the enjoyment of the fans is unsurpassed. It was always a pleasure to bump into Bill, who loved to talk to anyone about baseball, whether you bumped into him on the streets of Hyde Park, at his stool at Miller's Pub, or out in the bleachers at Wrigley Field.

To the current Sox owners, Jerry Reinsdorf, Eddie Einhorn, et al, who built an organization out of loyalty, staffed with the likes of Kenny Williams, Ozzie Guillen, Greg Walker, "Coop," "The Rock" Raines, Harold, Greg Walker, etc. that built us a solid championship team this year. To Ozzie Guillen, whose outstanding nurturing, leadership, and motivation turned the Sox clubhouse into a hotbed of quiet confidence and the home of a selfless team that played every day with the heart, soul, and guts of champions. The Sox don't look like any other MLB team today, either in their unique mix of baseball skills, or in spirit.

To the 2005 White Sox players, who struggled all year with a total lack of respect that continues even to this day after they went wire to wire in 1st place and swept 2 or 3 playoff opponents in one of the most impressive seasons by any team ever. May you relish in your victory and know in your hearts that you will be back.

To Frank Thomas, arguably the greatest right-handed hitter of all time, whose unambiguously HOFer career stretches back to the last days of Old Comiskey Park. At least Walter Payton got to play in his Super Bowl. Frank merely got to stand by in his ankle cast, quietly gracious and grateful as ever, as the Sox marched through their playoff victims. Here's to Frank playing in the 2006 playoffs in silver and black for the two-peat next year!

To the many Sox players and managers of the past, whose many years of invested Sox loyalties were paid off in spades with the 2005 championship. To Minnie, Chet, Dick Allen, Joe Horlen, Wilbur, "Blackjack," "Beltin' Bill" Melton, and others, way too many to mention. It was amazing to see Al Lopez in the stands, looking so great at 90 something during the World Series, just days before his death.

To the many Sox announcers over the years, particularly to the all-time most irreverent Jimmy Piersall and Harry Caray, but also to Jack Brickhouse, Hawk Harrelson, Tom Paciorak, DJ, and all the rest.

To Jim O'Donnell, who used to go to every opening day game with me (when we both still lived in Chicago), regardless of weather or work obligations every year. We suffered through many a rainy, frozen early April game, which no amount of consumed "anti-freeze" could overcome. I'm sure his old '62 Ford Falcon with the rusted-through seat mounts still has that old "Go Go White Sox" sticker in the windshield.

To the many families full of fanatical Sox fans I've shared the penitence of being a Sox fan with over the years: the Taylors, the Seahausens, the Sloweys, the Buists, the Jelens, and many others. To all the staff here at WSI and all the fanatical members (even all you "dark clouds"). Your wait is over and your team is now champions.

To the ghost of Old Comiskey Park, whose long history as one of the major icons of baseball, not only with the legacy of the Sox, but also as origin of the all-star game and home to many of the greatest games and players of the negro leagues, is unsurpassed.

—ode to veeck

Dedicated to ...my grandpa to be able to view a World Series winner in his lifetime. I thought about you when the last out was recorded. Celebrate, Grandpa; this one's for you!

—SoXPriDe33

Dedicated to ...**Chicago Sox fans.**

To me, words such as loyalty, respect, and honor have meaning that go beyond their definitions in a dictionary.

With that said, I dedicate this championship season to all Sox fans, past and present, from the great city of Chicago. It was *they* who stayed loyal and true to a team through the lean, difficult years, and it was their dedication that helped keep the Sox on the South Side. Chicagoans who've stayed the course with the Sox will always have my respect and gratitude. It was quite an honor to watch this team from the first pitch in spring training to the final out on October 26th.

Thank you.

—The Racehorse

Dedicated to . . .all the old-timer White Sox fans I used to see at Comiskey during the Lopez and Stanky years. Many kept meticulous scorecards while they cheered on their Sox. In their old age they were rewarded with one pennant and lots of "almost" years. They would have enjoyed this so much, and we Sox fans can never thank them enough for their long-term loyalty and devotion to an enterprise that was a cause just as much as their favorite baseball team.

To my father, who despite everything that happened between us is still the one responsible for me becoming a Chicago White Sox fan.

To my wife for being the only person to share this magical October with me in the alien landscape where we now reside.

Most of all, to the 2005 White Sox for not caring about or being intimidated by "history." For paving the way to a new exciting era of team play in the post steroids era. For making us all so relieved, proud, and oh so very happy. Go, go, go 2005 White Sox. Chicago is proud of you.

—PaulDrake

Dedicated to . . .my dad and two grandfathers; thank you for the wonderful memories at the old park. My mom and my uncle who taught me loyalty through the bad years, and God knows there were plenty of those. They told me stick with them because they are your team. Every April thinking this is the year. Well, finally it was our year; it was a great ride, and by the way, how about a couple more!!

—rjdmichjr

Dedicated to . . . every true White Sox fan I know or have known, who deserves this one and so many more. We waited our whole lives for this, and we all got to see it from one vantage point or another.

—ZachAL

Dedicated to . . . all those years spent watching losing baseball. To Joe Jackson, who was not quite bright enough to figure what he was getting into in 1919, and to Buck Weaver, who probably didn't deserve what he got. Most importantly, this is for Chicago, deprived of a World Series winner for 88 years. To the start of a dynasty not seen since Michael Jordan, this championship is dedicated to Kenny Williams and Ozzie Guillen for making this possible. Those two deserve the most credit out of anybody. Once again, thank you so much; this feels unreal, and I will savor it forever.

—minastirith67

Dedicated to . . . the City of Chicago and White Sox fans worldwide.

2005 Chicago White Sox, choking on celebratory cigar smoke.

—row18

Dedicated to …my "Yonder Father"—a true baseball man through and through. Lived and breathed the sport, but not always in your typical fashion. He loved statistics and bought Bill James' books religiously. Many times as a kid I would catch him deep in those books, hanging on every technical detail.

My most cherished memory of my dad was his constant belittling of Reggie Jackson. Not only did he consider him one of the biggest jerks to ever play the game, but reminded me, on MANY occasions, that yes, he did hit 563 HR in his career, but struck out 2,597 times! For those that don't know, this was an AMAZING stat since for years Willie Stargell, second place on the list, only had 1,936. Of course, now "Shamming Sammy" has amassed 2,194 Ks in his "enhanced" career to take over second place, something for me to howl about to my son!

For some reason, although he grew up in East Chicago, he was a loyal Reds fan. So although he passed on in 2003, at least he could enjoy a wire-to-wire title with his team in 1990.

I also dedicate this championship to my son, who thanks to this glorious run has become a RABID Sox fan, and I can't wait to start enjoying many WINNING years of White Sox baseball with him!

In addition, cheers to ALL you Sox fans, young and old, and those who have passed on before us for sticking with the team through some very thin years. Also my heartfelt gratitude to all those great WSI fans I met at Puffer's during those final, wonderful games.

Finally, thanks to the players who brought it home. You have forever rid this generation of living with the stigma of another stat that always astounded my dad—SO many years without any championships for BOTH Chicago teams! Watching you during the playoffs was at times stressful and almost unbearable, but in the end I have nothing but SWEET memories to savor the rest of my days.

GO GO WHITE SOX; WE ARE ALL PROUD OF YOU!!!

—IronFisk

Dedicated to . . .my dad, a huge Sox fan, and the reason why I am who I am today in so many ways. He took me to my first Sox game (at least that I can remember), a 1984 affair against the Seattle Mariners. We bought a pennant of the 1983 Division winning team that still hangs in my bedroom. I can still remember seeing the glow from the lights over the park the first time we walked up the stairs to the field level. The rest of that decade was spent at many a "perfect attendance" night at a half-empty ballpark. I remember being at our last game at Old Comiskey, which also happened to be Bobby Thigpen's 50th save of his record-setting season. The '90s were filled with many opening day contests and a slew of Sox/Indians match-ups. And, I'm sure, more Sox games than he ever could have expected during the 1997 season. Even while I was at college, the Sox provided a link that kept us in consistent communication throughout the year. We were at Game 2 of the 2000 ALDS together, which, of course, didn't go as we hoped. Because of him I was able to attend Game 2 of the ALCS and Game 1 of the World Series this year. I'll never, ever forget those games. He coached me all throughout Little League, taught me to love the game, and took me to more White Sox games than I can count. So, this is for my dad. You've been waiting about 24 years longer for this than I have—I hope it was even better than you thought it would be. Go White Sox!

—**Scot Bertram**

CPSIA information can be obtained
at www.ICGtesting.com
Printed in the USA
LVOW11s0231041116

511415LV00001B/10/P

9 781425 901875